LIFE'S LORDSHIP OVER DEATH

A Study of Immortality and the Hereafter From a Wesleyan Perspective

Charles W. Carter's Published Books

Transformed Africans (Wesleyan Methodist Publishing Association, 1938).

A Half Century of American Wesleyan Missions in West Africa (Wesleyan Methodist Publishing Association, 1940).

The Bible Gift of Tongues (Wesleyan Methodist Publishing Association, 1951).

Road To Revival (Higley Publishing Company, 1959).

The Acts of the Apostles: Co-authored with Ralph Earle (Zondervan Publishing House, 1959; reprinted by Schmul Publishing Company as *A Schmul Commentary,* 1973).

Christian Songs in Temne: Co-authored with George Hemminger (General Council-Assemblies of God, 1949).

Evangelical Sunday School Commentary (Higley Press, 1960).

Evangelical Sunday School Commentary (Higley Press, 1961).

Evangelical Sunday School Lesson Commentary (Higley Press, 1960).

Evangelical Sunday School Lesson Commentary (Higley Press, 1961).

The Wesleyan Bible Commentary, 6 Vols., Gen. Ed. and author of *Acts, Ephesians, 1 Corinthians, Hebrews* and *Book of Job* (Eerdmans, 1964; reprinted and published by Hendrickson Publishers, Inc., 1986).

The Holy Spirit in the Early Church (Published in Chinese by the Church of the Nazarene Mission, Taipei, Taiwan, 1974).

Ethics: From Pagan To Christian (Published in Chinese by the Oriental Missionary Society in Taiwan, 1972).

The Person and Ministry of the Holy Spirit: A Wesleyan Perspective (Baker Book House, 1974: Reprinted by Schmul Publishing Co., Inc., 1983).

The Wesleyan Theological Journal, Ed. and contributor 1965-72 (Published by the Wesleyan Theological Society).

Missionaries Extraordinary: The Life and Labors of Charles and Elizabeth Carter (Published by the author, 1982).

A Contemporary Wesleyan Theology: Biblical, Systematic and Practical. 2 Vols., Gen. Ed. and author of three and a half chapters; "Anthropology," "Hamartiology," "Judeo-Christian Ethics," and co-author of the "Divine Mandate," with Dr. Everette N. Hunt (Zondervan Publishing House, 1983).

From Revival To Evangelism (Harold E. Schmul Publishing Company, Inc., 1986).

Life's Lordship Over Death (Wesley Press, 1988).

Contributor to various published books, scholarly journals, periodicals, including *The Zondervan Pictorial Encyclopedia of the Bible* (Zondervan Publishing House, 1975) 5 Vols; *Beacon Dictionary of Theology* (Beacon Hill Press, 1983).

LIFE'S LORDSHIP OVER DEATH

A Study of Immortality and the Hereafter From a Wesleyan Perspective

Dr. Charles W. Carter

Wesley Press
Indianapolis, Indiana

Dedication

With deep appreciation and sincere affection the author dedicates this volume to the more than twelve thousand students who have sat in his classes during the past forty-five years at the following institutions: Clarke Memorial Biblical Seminary in Sierra Leone Africa; Marion College; Taylor University; West Indies Bible College in Barbados; Oriental Missionary Society Theological College in Taiwan; Union Biblical Seminary in Medellin, Colombia, S.A.; China Evangelical Seminary in Taipei, Taiwan; Union Biblical Seminary in India; and Kingsley College in Australia. These classes have consisted of Systematic Theology; Ethics; Logic; Philosophy; Contemporary Theology; Bible; Hermeneutics; Homiletics; Psychology of Religion; Pneumatology; Cultural Anthropology; Wesleyan History; and Christian World Missions.

Table of Contents

Foreword

Dr. Charles W. Carter is a renowned scholar read throughout the world of evangelical Christianity. He has an impressive record of writing and teaching over a period of fifty years. The first of over twenty works he has written or edited was published in 1938. Reprinted numerous times and best known among all his contributions are *The Wesleyan Bible Commentary* in six volumes, *The Acts of the Apostles,* co-authored with Dr. Ralph Earle; *The Person and Ministry of the Holy Spirit: A Wesleyan Perspective,* and more recently, *A Contemporary Wesleyan Theology* in two volumes.

The publication of *Life's Lordship Over Death* will enrich one's understanding and appreciation for God's total provision for the whole of His universe. The book's readers will include college and university professors, students, ministers and teachers, as well as lay people who have wished for a treatment of the subjects included herein. This work is ideally suited for reading and discussion by Bible study groups that frequently want something substantial to read along with the Scriptures and which will cause them to think about death and immortality.

Charles W. Carter was one of the very first Wesleyan scholars I ever heard in a lecture series given 40 years ago when I was an undergraduate student. His engaging manner and deliberate choice of weighty, meaningful words are as intriguing now in written form as they were then in spoken oratory. Undeniably the subjects of this book are, and should be, of vital interest to every Christian believer. It is my prayer that this publication will be the springboard for many inspiring discussions as readers contemplate their own temporality and futurity.

In the context of ancient pagan and modern non-Christian philosophies of death compared to Old Testament views, Dr. Carter makes a strong point that death is not corrective in purpose or result. Death is the natural outcome of the Fall, not punishment for disobedience.

Punishment is corrective in purpose. Death does not imply arbitrary punishment for sin. Those lost in hell are not being punished, for in that place there is no hope of correction. Death was God's means of stopping the progressive degeneration of any one person. It is the end of temporal existence.

The author shows that the Old Testament concept of death is generally collective, while in the New Testament death is personal and individual. Moral evil and the devil are the cause of death for Paul and are so shown in other parts of the New Testament. Even natural, impersonal creation has fallen under the curse of a universal moral law, bringing destruction and havoc to God's order of things. Even so, the impersonal creation will share in the redemptive provision of Christ ultimately.

Dr. Carter does not see the present world of order being annihilated. Nothing God made is destroyed, for annihilation implies nothingness. The recycling, conversion or change of elements from one form to another does not mean the end of those elements. Isaiah, Daniel, Paul and others agree with this conclusion.

Believers experience transitional change but physical, social, marital death are all perversions of humanity's moral sense. For the Christian the spiritual law of life transcends the natural moral law of sin and death.

The doctrine of hell, its nature and significance,

with biblical or nonbiblical views of the second death, the intermediate state, universalism, soul sleep, and annihilation as an emphasis of the cults are explored by the author, as he shows that conscious, spiritual existence following physical death is a biblical teaching. Spiritism is described as pan-psychic monism. Communication with the dead (necromancy), in the seance via a medium, is illustrated by references to Bishop James Pike, literary works of the New Age Movement, and the Witch of Endor.

Dr. Carter does not avoid some of the tough problems, but delves with alacrity into the Roman Catholic belief in purgatory. They teach that it is both a place and a state where the souls of the dead suffer for pardonable, venial sins which have not been cared for in life; but purgatory has no remedy for mortal sins. Those who are still living offer effectual prayers for the dead and some even add the view that the dead offer prayers for the living.

Purgatory is preparation for heaven and a means for the priestly control of the whole scheme of penance, indulgences and absolution. It is seen from Intertestamental Apocryphal literature and that of the early Church Fathers, that the justice of God demanded a post-mortem purging if heaven was to be attained.

In the development of the doctrine the Councils of Florence and Trent also affirmed such teaching, which links purgatory with the Roman Catholic concepts of sin and salvation. Man is capable of and responsible for completing his own salvation by means of suffering here and hereafter. God requires this for balancing accounts. In all fairness Dr. Carter gives considerable attention both to the positive benefits and negative criticisms of purgatory.

The book comes alive with graphic imagery drawn from numerous sources in the author's fascinating account of life everlasting and in his views of Christian immortality. Immortality is defined as the survival of the soul or personality in post-physical consciousness. Dr. Carter discounts the idea of creationism as an explanation for the origin of the soul or personality. God's original creative act was that of creating Adam as an everlasting conscious personality, capable of procreating himself in the traducianistic views of Augustine, body, soul and personality.

The great majority of publications on the subject of immortality reflect only a superficial acquaintance with such other concepts of futurity as pre-existence, transmigration of souls, karma, or annihilation of the wicked. All these views are rejected, of course, in favor of Christian immortality. The validity, necessity and necessary grounds for Christian immortality are carefully outlined and discussed by the author.

Few of Dr. Carter's students will ever forget his penchant for careful, logical, sequential presentation of any subject he undertook to discuss. This is no less true in his writings and in the present work as he systematically leads the reader to think about the everlasting moral freedom of human personality, the rational consciousness, moral responsibility, the indestructibility of the soul, the improvability of personality, and the existence of an infinite moral sphere, all of which give evidence for the necessity of immortality.

Dr. Carter engages the reader in his final chapter with the topics of heaven and the hereafter. Intriguing questions such as the following are addressed: Where is heaven? What will be the character of heaven? Will there be activity in heaven? The answers to these questions can open broad vistas of one's future here as well as hereafter.

Without a doubt from biblical evidence heaven will be a state in which there is the absence of all that is negative and evil — sin, Satan, temptation, sorrow, pain, tears, death — while it is the presence of all purity and glory, the wonders of devotion and worship, where personalities are glorified, purified and exalted in motive and purpose.

All humanity with all creation will be restored to God's original purpose and perfection as intended before the Fall. Above all, heaven will be characterized by love. Nothing of value in God's natural created order or the divine humanly achieved values throughout history will be lost when God's redemptive plan is completed. God's universe will be restored to perfection in the completion of the divine redemptive scheme. Christ will have complete victory over the entire universe.

Moreover, those who are redeemed by Christ will have their part in Christ's authority over His redeemed order. He will reign in conjunction with His redeemed followers until God's purpose for the whole universe before the Fall is restored, purified, perfected and fulfilled. In God's redemptive provision in Christ the final consummation will be realized in *Life's Lordship Over Death!*

Wayne E. Caldwell, Th.D.
General Editor
The Wesleyan Church

Preface

Why a book on *Life's Lordship Over Death,* rather than Christ's victory over death through His cross and resurrection? At the outset, it is generally recognized that all sincere Christian believers accept without question Christ's resurrection victory over death with its eventual provisions for the resurrection of mankind from the dead. This hardly requires further evidence for Christian believers. Second, the moral trends and events of recent times have tended to cast a pall of pessimism over the consciousness of modern society, to which even many Christian believers have fallen victims. The minds of contemporary humanity have been bombarded by the media with reports of crime, immorality, revolutions, wars, human tragedies, dishonesties in business and governments and the failures of modern society in general, to the extent that the conscience and hopes of many people have been dulled, if not deadened to the future hope for mankind.

Again, recent decades have witnessed the revival of secular humanism which has made its inroads into every area of life and thought. Much of modern thinking has been caught up in contemporary secular humanism in the areas of science, environmentalistic determinism in sociology, psychology, psychiatry, and for some, even civilization itself. Such great minds as Albert Schweitzer, Arnold Toynbee and P. A. Sorokin have concluded that modern civilization is declining, and will continue to do so unless there is to be a recovery of reverence for life and an ethical sense. Thus humanity has been reduced to a victim rather than a victor over the natural creation, as God had originally planned and decreed (Gen. 1:26-28). Likewise much of contemporary Christianity has failed to escape the devastating effects of this enervating thought climate.

In the 1960s religious secularism came to its climax in the "God is Dead Theology" with the works of such world-renowned thinkers as Bishop John Robinson's *Honest To God* (concerning which C. S. Lewis remarked that "he would rather be honest *with* God"), and Thomas Altizer's *The Gospel of Christian Atheism,* to mention but two of the many works of this era. With "God dead and buried" all moral foundations disappeared and "ethical situationism" consequently replaced biblical morality.

Upon the heels of this dilemma has followed the breakdown of the home, disrespect for human life, widespread drug addiction, riots, rampant criminality, revolutions, wars and the serious threat of anarchy in which society would destroy itself. Consequently, stark pessimism concerning the future stalks the minds of vast numbers of people. The cry of many today, as with the ancient prophet, is "Watchman, what of the night?" (Isa. 21:11 KJV).

However, there is another side to the coin of history and the contemporary situation. That other side has been eloquently expressed by the Apostle Paul, who himself lived through the dark days of the decline of pagan Roman civilization. In the face of that unprecedented situation he confidently declared, "We know that in everything God works for good with those who love him, who are called according to his purpose" (Rom. 8:28 RSV). Though Paul is not saying that God rules and controls all that occurs in life and human history, he is giving assurance that God will *ultimately overrule* the evil and bring His purposes and plans to their divinely predetermined ends.

It is the thesis of this book that God is providentially accomplishing His purpose for His entire created order, notwithstanding the death-dealing effects that the Fall, Satan, and sin have wrought in the universe. Three possible attitudes may be assumed in life and its outlook on the future, today or in any day. One is "stark pessimism" in which all hope is lost. This is well expressed by the nihilistic philosophy of Bertrand Russell of England when he says that all is "destined to extinction in the vast death of the solar system, and that the whole temple of man's achievement must inevitably be buried beneath the debris of a universe in ruins — . . . [and] that no philosophy which rejects them can hope to stand."

Another position is "blind optimism," such as is expressed by Robert Browning, that "God is on His throne and all is well with the world," a half-truth at best. Certainly God is on His throne, but is all well with the world? Only a color-blind optimist would conclude thus. However, there is a third position, which is the position of the author of this book. That position is "Christian realism." It is well expressed by the prophet Isaiah in one of the darkest periods of Israel's history in "the year that king Uzziah died." The prophet's faith penetrated the inky blackness of that overshadowing, threatening cloud that enshrouded the nation, and with an exclamation of hope declared, "I saw [also] the Lord seated on a throne, high and exalted" (Isa. 6:1 NIV). In Christian realism the worst may and must be faced and frankly acknowledged. But then with confidence in an all-wise and all-powerful God we may see God working out His plan and purpose for mankind and His created order for their final restoration to and beyond the perfection in which He originally created them. This is the author's position. The following homely couplet well expresses the difference between the outlook of the pessimist and the realistic optimist:

Two prisoners looked out through prison bars,
One saw mud and the other saw stars.

Or again, in a similar vein, another unknown writer has advised:

As you travel on through life, Brother,
Whatever be your Goal,
Keep your eye upon the doughnut,
And not upon the hole!

It should be noted that all copyrighted quotations in this book are duly acknowledged and documented in the End Notes of each chapter. Unless otherwise indicated, the Scripture quotations used in this book are from the *New American Standard Bible;* La Habra, California; The Lockman Foundation, 1960, 1962, 1963, 1968, 1971. For these and all other quotations in this work the author expresses his indebtedness.

Likewise, the author wishes to express his indebtedness and sincere appreciation to Dr. Wayne E. Caldwell, General Editor of The Wesleyan Church, and his efficient editorial assistant, Mrs. Alberta Metz, for their encouragement and untiring efforts in bringing this work to an acceptable condition for publication. To Mr. Mark Batman, General Publisher of The Wesleyan Church, the author likewise expresses his gratitude for the decision to undertake the production of this work as a publication of Wesley Press. Not least is the author's indebtedness to several Christian scholars who read the manuscript of this work prior to its publication, offered helpful criticisms, and wrote their brief evaluations of the manuscript. These include Drs. Ralph Earle, J. D. Abbott, Richard S. Taylor, David L. McKenna, Donald E. Demaray, and Lt. Col. Henry Gariepy. To Teresa Daugherty, the author's secretary, he wishes to express sincere appreciation for her faithful work in typing the manuscript.

That the author has not made explicit many of the implications of his position herein expressed will be evident to the reader. That this is due in part to the limitations of space will be appreciated, as also in part to his respect for the intelligence of the readers. However, it is hoped that the alert reader will grasp the significance of the implications as well as the explicitly stated positions of the author. If this book inspires in the minds and lives of the readers a renewed degree of optimism and hope for humanity and the universe in the outworking of God's redemptive plan through Jesus Christ, that will be the author's greatest reward. With a sincere prayer to that end this work is sent forth to the reading public.

Charles W. Carter
Marion, Indiana, 1988

Chapter I
The Universal Law of Life Over Death

Introduction

Two divinely established universal laws are operating in the universe. The one is natural moral law; the other is supernatural law. From the natural moral law perspective comes the law of sin and death. The supernatural law is the law of righteousness and life. Each person must choose by which law he or she will live. The consequences go with the choices of each.

Natural moral law was established by God and functions automatically by cause and effect, expressing the established justice of God. God's supernatural law functions according to His direct personal will, expressing His justice, love and mercy through divine intervention into the realm of natural law. God's natural law is His regular way of governing. His supernatural law is His higher way of exercising His sovereignty. That God sometimes intervenes in the process of the outworking of the natural law, in answer to the prayers of His people, or the exercise of His mysterious providence, as in the case of dangerous debilitating diseases or tragic accidents, is clear from both human experience and the Scriptures.

Likewise God sometimes uses natural means to accomplish His supernatural purposes, as when Jesus Christ healed the blind man with clay and spittle (John 9:6-12), or when God sent a strong wind to divide the Red Sea that allowed the Israelites to cross over on dry ground (Exod. 14:21-22). Likewise the anointing of the sick with oil, in accompaniment with the prayers of the elders for healing, is understood by many scholars to represent medicinal rather than sacramental use (James 5:14-15). That God works through modern medicine for the restoration of the sick few would deny, and those who deny this fall into fanatical and sometimes criminal practices. God is the God of nature as well as of the supernatural. John Wesley recognized this fact and often prescribed natural remedies in accompaniment with prayers for the sick; and Wesley has been judged to have been as well qualified as most of the physicians of his day, and even better than many of them, according to Dr. David Stewart, M.D. (cf. *Wesleyan Theological Journal,* Vol. 4, No. 1, 1969, pp. 27-38).

An important factor seldom recognized is that neither medicine nor surgery are actually curative. They are designed to either prevent or eliminate the factors or conditions that inhibit health and wholeness in the organism, and thus allow natural law and God to restore that organism to normality. This is one of the reasons that nursing care is often more effective in medical practice for the restoration of health than either medicine or surgery. This is not, however, to minimize the importance of medicine or surgery. It is rather to note their realm of effectiveness in medical practice as being negative rather than positive. Medicine may prevent or eliminate, but it is nature and God that heal and restore health. Medicine is God ordained and extremely important, and to medical science society owes a heavy debt.

Humanistic, naturalistic science says that the universe is a closed causal system and that all creation, including mankind, is locked into that closed causal system — that cause and effect determine all that occurs in the universe and the life of humanity.

Christian faith recognizes the existence and function of the natural moral law as established by God for the normal government of all creation. That there are, however, certain humanly unexplainable variations and disfunctions in the natural order is evident. That these variations are sometimes due to human error, greed, or even possible demonical interferences is likewise evident. The latter is especially evident in the Book of Job (Job 1:9-19; 2:7), and from the declaration of the Apostle Paul (Eph. 2:2; 6:12). On the other hand, such occurrences as the Three Mile Island nuclear plant malfunction in Pennsylvania in 1978 illustrate the hazards of human error in the malfunction of natural law, as do nuclear waste deposits that endanger human health and life. Or, as in nature's malfunction in the 1985 earthquake in Mexico City that left countless victims dead and untold property damage; or the eruption of Mount Dea Ruiz Volcano near Bogota, Colombia, that buried an entire city and killed more than twenty-five thousand people, to cite only a few examples.

The devastating effects of the dust storms in the western United States in the 1930s resulted, in large measure, from the overworked soil of those regions, motivated by human greed for financial gain. The human result of this devastation provided the setting for Steinbeck's famous book, *Grapes of Wrath*.

That there are instances of demonical interference causing disruptions in the normal functions of natural law the Bible seems to give clear evidence. Such was the case in the experiences of Job (see Job, chapters 1 and 2). The Apostle Paul refers to Satan as *"the prince of the power of the air . . . the spirit that is now working in the sons of disobedience"* (Eph. 2:2). Again, he says the Christian's "struggle is . . . against the rulers, against the powers, against the world-forces of this darkness, against the spiritual *forces of wicked-ness in the heavenly places"* (Eph. 6:12).

That such malfunctions are traceable ultimately to the moral evil inherent in the Fall is both scriptural and reasonable. These and innumerable other natural disasters are related to and often productive of damage or physical death to humanity, as also the disruption of life in other areas of God's originally ordered creation. They reflect the consequences, through the Fall, of the alienation from God of humanity, whom He had placed over His created order (Gen. 1:26-30; cf. Rom. 8:19-22). The Apostle Paul said: "This, then, is what has happened. Sin made its entry into the world through one man, and through sin, death. The entail of sin and death passed on to the whole human race, and no one could break it for no one was himself free from sin" (Rom. 5:12 *Phillips*). "The wages of sin is death" (Rom. 6:23).

Christian faith, however, recognizes also the supernatural law as higher and greater than natural law. Both are the laws of God, but the supernatural transcends and has power to contravene the natural. For this reason the Quaker philosopher, Elton Trueblood, says, "Ours is, indeed, in some sense an open universe."[1] There is always room in God's universe for answered prayer, miracles, and divine intervention.

The naturalistic concept of a closed, cause-effect mechanical universe operating independently of God and His supernatural law was the deistic view of the late seventeenth and eighteenth centuries. Likewise this view is closely allied with, if not identical to, the contemporary view of humanistic, naturalistic science.

Under the law of nature, any violation of that law has its inevitable consequence. All sin, or moral evil, is a violation of God's natural law, as also His supernatural law. The result of this is a perversion of His natural law and the misdirection of life, resulting in self-destruction and ultimately death itself for humanity, unless there are repentance and faith.

Since the Fall, unregenerate mankind has never been able, without the help of God, to live harmoniously with God's established moral order, or His natural law. Sin has been the universal experience of humanity, and spiritual death has been the universal consequence. Death, then, takes its place among the universal experiences of mankind. The Bible declares that "it is appointed for men to die once" (Heb. 9:27), or as the NIV has it, "man is destined to die once." The certainty of physical death is made explicit in this latter translation. Death is the inescapable *destiny* of all humanity, and physical death is a *onetime* experience for all mankind. Viewed from a *natural* perspective, death is a one-way route from which there is no return. Thus if considered naturally, death for humanity is universal, inescapable, irresistible, and irreversible.

In its root meaning, death signifies *separation*. Formally defined, physical death means "the total and permanent cessations of all the vital functions of an animal [person] or plant" (*Random House Dictionary*). Spiritual death, however, means "the loss or absence of spiritual life" (RHD), or separation from God who is the only source of spiritual life.

The Greek Concept of Death

The basic secular Greek word for death is *thanatos.* W. Schmithals states that with Homer *thanatos* (death) "means the act of dying or the state of death. But it is also used of mortal danger, the manner of death, and the death penalty."[2] Schmithals says further that in the Hellenist period the term *thanatos,* and its derivatives, were used metaphorically of intellectual and spiritual death. For the Greeks, he states:

> Death meant the end of living activity, the closing of the life-span, the destruction of existence. . . .
> Death is the common destiny of man . . . . Realization of the inevitability of death found its normal

consequence in the demand to enjoy life . . . to the full. The maxim cited by Paul in 1 Cor. 15:32, "Let us eat and drink, for tomorrow we die," accords with many expressions of Greek and Roman thought on the matter . . . Roman dining rooms of the imperial period sometimes had pictures of a skeleton with the inscription "Know thyself." This is an invitation to make sure not to miss the pleasures of the moment.[3]

Plato (427?-347 B.C.) and Spinoza at a much later time (1632-1677) held opposing views on one's attitude toward death. As recorded by Frederick D. Kershner, Plato taught,

The wise man . . . is the one who has constantly before him the certainty of death, while the modern philosopher [Spinoza] says that there is nothing which the truly wise man will think about so little as his approaching demise.[4]

Kershner is doubtless correct in stating that "something can be said for both points of view. If we have entered into the divine life while here, we may be well assured that we shall be sharers in that life hereafter."[5]

Plato, while neither Jew nor Christian, seems to have come close to belief in a personal God. As a pagan Greek, however, he shared something of the morbid Hellenistic concept of death as the finality of life. Spinoza, on the other hand, while a Jew by religion, was a systematic pantheist who thought of the soul as only a mode (or manifestation) of the all-pervasive impersonal spirit of the universe. With death the soul, or quasi spiritual personality of man, would be dissolved into the impersonal, pantheistic Universal All. Thus Spinoza's philosophy had no place for personal immortality in the hereafter. The same can be said for Aristotle (384-322 B.C.).

The Old Testament Concept of Death

Thanatos (Gr. death) and its cognates constitute

the words for death in the Septuagint version of the Old Testament. The Hebrew equivalent of these terms is, for the most part, *māivet* (death), or *mût* (to die, or kill).

The Old Testament meaning of death sometimes seems to signify the final end of man's existence (2 Sam. 14:14). As his body is from the earth it is destined, since the Fall, to return to dust (Gen. 3:19). In his fallen state man is separated from God who is the source of life and therefore he is left without hope beyond the present existence (Pss. 6:5; 30:9; 88:5, 10-12; Isa. 38:11-12). There is no alternative to death in this view (Gen. 3:19). Long life and temporal prosperity with male posterity to carry on the name and the family line is the general view of the Old Testament (Gen. 15:15; Ps. 91:16).

There are, however, certain exceptions to the foregoing view of death in the Old Testament. Some sort of continued existence in the afterlife is suggested by the oft-repeated expression in the Old Testament that indicates a community of the dead. This was spoken of Abraham: "Abraham breathed his last and died in a ripe old age, an old man and satisfied with life; and he *was gathered to his people*" (Gen. 25:8). Likewise, "Ishmael [after 137 years] breathed his last and died, and *was gathered to his people*" (Gen. 25:17). Also "Isaac breathed his last and died, and *was gathered to his people,* an old man of ripe age" (Gen. 35:29). Jacob said, "I am about to be *gathered to my people;* bury me with my fathers in the cave that is in the field of Ephron the Hittite" (Gen. 49:29). And "Jacob . . . breathed his last, and was *gathered to his people*" (Gen. 49:33). "Aaron will be *gathered to his people,* and will die there" (Num. 20:26). "You too shall be *gathered to your people,* as Aaron your brother was" (Num. 27:13). (See also Num. 31:2; Deut. 32:50; Judg. 2:10; 2 Kings 22:20; 2 Chron. 34:28; Job 19:25-27; Jer. 25:33).

However, there are also more hopeful glimpses of the life beyond the present in certain instances in the Old Testament. Out of the depth of his misery and suffering Job exultantly exclaimed: "As for me, I know that my Redeemer lives, and at the last He will take His stand on the earth. Even after my skin is flayed, yet without my flesh I shall see God; whom I myself shall behold, and whom my eyes shall see and not another" (Job 19:25-27).

Perhaps the clearest statement in the Old Testament concerning the future state of the dead, of both the righteous and the unrighteous, is given in The Book of Daniel. Confidently Daniel affirms: "Everyone who is found written in the book, will be rescued. And many of those who sleep in the dust of the ground will awake, these to everlasting life, but the others to disgrace and everlasting contempt [abhorrence]" (Dan. 12:1-2).

In one of God's first pronouncements to the progenitors of the human family He declared that disobedience to His explicit command would issue in death (Gen. 2:16-17). They violated that command and consequently died spiritually. They were separated from God who was the source of their vital spiritual life, with all that life provided and promised for their spiritual, moral, and temporal welfare. The light of their spiritual life was extinguished and they were left to wander in the fearful uncertainty of darkness. They became disoriented and woefully lost. They had no moral or spiritual frame of reference in their alienated condition. In their guilty hopelessness they tried in vain to hide themselves from their God from whom they had separated themselves by breach of their covenant relationship with Him. In the day they ate the forbidden fruit, they died spiritually. Like the sea captain who wrecks his vessel on the rocks of disaster, and takes his cargo, crew and passengers to their watery graves with him, so our foreparents sank the human race and all natural creation in the dark waters of death's night where they were separated from their Creator and Sustainer. They died and with them the entire human race died spiritually. "By one man sin entered the world, and death by sin; and so death passed upon all men, for that all have sinned" (Rom. 5:12 KJV). Under the moral law of nature all men are spiritually dead in their trespasses and sins (Eph. 2:1).

Death in the Old Testament, as also in the New, is the result, and thus a consequent of humanity's sin in the Fall, rather than a divine arbitrary punishment for that sin. Punishment, properly considered, has as its purpose *correction.* Inadequate as are the penal institutions, established by society and nations, in their inability to correct and rehabilitate criminals, such is nevertheless their purpose. The term *capital punishment* is a misnomer, for it means death, and death affords no correction for the condemned criminal. Whatever one's position, pro or con, on this issue, it is *execution* of the criminal rather than *punishment.* There is no correction in death. Likewise the state of the doomed is not, properly speaking, a state of punishment, as there is no hope of correction in that state, unless one believes in a *second-chance salvation,* or universalism with William Barclay or others of that school of thought. God instituted death to prevent the endless perpetuation of life in the progressive degeneracy and accumulation of evil in humanity's fallen state. Death was designed as a stop-gap to evil in humanity's temporal existence.

In His mercy, however, God provided redemption from death for all who die in faith in that provision (Pss. 30:3; 16:10). Though the passage may have messianic implications, as well as meaning for the believer, the psalmist asserts his confidence in God: "My heart is glad and my tongue rejoices; my body also will rest secure, because you will not abandon me to the grave, nor will you let your Holy One see decay" (Ps. 16:9-10 NIV).

The supposed exceptions to the universality of

death in the Old Testament are in considerable doubt. Concerning Enoch the Bible simply states, "Enoch was taken up so that he should not see death; and he was not found because God took him up; for he obtained the witness that before his being taken up he was pleasing to God" (Heb. 11:5). The Genesis record simply states that "Enoch walked with God; and he was not, for God took him" (Gen. 5:24). It is not stated how God took Enoch.

In the first place, whatever happened to Enoch was a result of his faith — "By faith Enoch" (Heb. 11:5). His translation, whatever it was, became a subjective fact with Enoch, by reason of the life of faith that he lived in God. His spiritual union with God through the obedience of faith was such that he shared the very eternal life of God himself, and consequently death could not conquer him, hidden as he was in God.

Withal, a correct understanding of this incident, in relation to the author's purpose in including it in the faith chapter of Hebrews, seems clearly to be that faith transcends death for the righteous. It suggests the completion of the redemptive work of faith in Christ, from man's lost state through the Fall, as the beginning of that redemptive work was exemplified in Enoch's justifying faith (v. 5). Enoch's faith was exhibited in his daily and uninterrupted walk with God across the stage of time for 365 years (Gen. 5:23). At the end of what men call temporal existence, his engagement with God was such that he seems not even to have been aware of the instant when he broke the sound barrier of temporal limitations and entered the limitlessness of spiritual outer space. So engrossed was he with God that he seems not to have been aware of the instant when his time-worn earthly garments of flesh fell away and he was clothed in his imperishable celestial space-suit (cf. 2 Cor. 5:1-9).

No funeral services were conducted on the occasion of Enoch's decease, by reason of the fact that his body could not be found: "he was not found, because God translated him." Perhaps God interred his physical remains in a secret sepulcher to await the resurrection of the righteous, as He did the body of Moses (cf. Deut. 34:5-6). However, the exemplary life that Enoch lived on earth among men has never been forgotten. One rendering says that before his decease "he received testimony [still on record] that he pleased and had been satisfactory to God" (Heb. 11:5 ANT). Enoch experienced and exemplified by faith that which is the highest and most earnest desire of every man in his sober and reflective moments, as that desire is so well expressed by J. B. Phillips, "We want our transitory life to be absorbed into the Life that is eternal" (2 Cor. 5:4).

However, whether it is allowed that he passed imperceptibly through the experience of death, or that he never experienced death at all, the meaning is quite the same. The author means to say that faith in God ultimately abrogates, or destroys, the real meaning of death (1 Cor. 15:54-57), and that Enoch was such a man of faith. Furthermore, he suggests that in the transcendent faith of Enoch we have the ultimate certainty of the resurrection and immortality of all true believers (cf. Ps. 23:4).

In his conversation with Martha on the occasion of Lazarus' death, Jesus specifically declared himself to be "the resurrection and the life." And then He asserted, "The man who believes in Me will live even though he dies, and anyone who is alive and believes in Me will never die at all" (John 11:25-26 *Phillips*). The psalmist realized this great truth that Enoch experienced and exemplified, and likewise declared that faith transcends death. "Even though I walk through the valley of the shadow of death, I fear no evil; for Thou art with me; . . . And I will dwell in the house of the Lord forever" (Ps. 23:4a, 6b). So then Enoch exemplifies the faith that pleases God and procures immortality.[6]

Perhaps as much may be said for the case of Elijah, though under different circumstances (2 Kings 2:1-12). The experience of death has lost its significance for many like Enoch and Elijah whose walk with God sublimated the experience of death (Ps. 23:4).

The New Testament Concept of Death

The Greek term for death (*thanatos*) occurs about 120 times in the New Testament. In the Gospels it most frequently applies to Christ's own death, whereas in Paul's writings it refers mainly to human death.

While there is continuity in the use of the term *death* from the Old Testament to the New, in the Old Testament physical death is generally regarded as collective while in the New it is individualistic. Continuing community life in the hereafter does not appear in the New Testament in the same manner as it does in the Old. At all times the reality of personal death is clear and certain throughout the New Testament.

Paul states clearly that moral evil (sin) is the basic cause of death. He declares that "the wages of sin is death" (Rom. 6:23). The author of Hebrews assigns authority over death to Satan as the instigator of sin and death, when he speaks of "him who had the power of death, that is, the devil" (Heb. 2:14), though his power was broken by Christ. Paul is concerned with death as a theological and moral issue rather than biological. This is evident in his concern with the universality of sin as moral evil and its consequent guilt. Sin severs humanity's relationship with the source of spiritual life and thus separates man spiritually from that source of life (Rom. 4:17). Severed from his relationship with God man falls under the moral law of nature by which he exists as a subject of natural law in divorcement from God. Since the law can never produce life, man is made the subject of slavery to sin and the object of death. Paul said, "The letter of the Law leads to the death of the soul; the Spirit of God alone can give the soul life" (2 Cor. 3:6 *Phillips).* The unitary nature of man renders him a psycho-physical being who, in alienation from God, is subject to death in his total being. In recognition of this fact Paul cries out, "Who will set me free from the body of this death?" (Rom. 7:24).

Upon the return of the prodigal son his father said, "This son of mine *was dead,* and has come to life again" (Luke 15:24). To his elder son the father said, "This brother of yours *was dead* and has begun to live" (Luke 15:32). The younger son's separation from his father and family had rendered him dead to that relationship, which signifies in this parable the spiritual death of humanity in divorcement from the Heavenly Father.

Likewise, John, in the fourth Gospel, recognizes the reality of death as set in opposition to life in Christ, the giver of life. Jesus declared, "Truly, truly, I say to you, he who hears My word, and believes Him who sent Me . . . has passed out of death into life" (John 5:24). Again, in words suggesting Enoch's experience, Jesus says, "Truly, truly, I say to you, if anyone keeps My word he shall *never see death"* (John 8:51). Jesus does not say that such a person will not die, but rather that death will lose its meaning for such a one. This is clarified in the Lazarus account where Jesus states that He is the resurrection and the life, and that "he who believes in Me shall live *even* if he dies," and He then adds, "Everyone who lives and believes in Me shall never die" (John 11:25-26).

The Disruption of Nonhuman Creation
in Relation to Humanity's Death

We are not left without an answer to the problem of universal death in the natural universe. At the completion of creation God gave to man the responsibility of sub-sovereignty over the natural created order (Gen. 1:27-30). This awesome responsibility gave to humanity power over all of the natural creation. Since all life issues ultimately from God, the very breath of life that vitalizes nature is dependent upon God. When man, as lord over God's natural creation, severed his relationship with God in the Fall, he not only subjected himself to the resultant death, but he likewise subjected the totality of his God-given natural realms to disruption. As previously noted, man, as captain of the ship which he sank through disobedience to his Commander, took with him to its watery grave the totality of nature aboard that vessel.

Paul treats this issue thus: "The creation was subjected to futility [meaninglessness], not of its own will, but because of Him who subjected it" (Rom. 8:20). There is a twofold meaning in the subjection of natural creation to futility. By reason of God's pronouncement of death upon man's disobedience while he was lord of natural creation, that creation fell with man under the curse of the universal moral law and suffered disruption. On the other hand, man as God's delegated lord over all creation was responsible for subjecting created nature to futility by his violation of God's command. In either case, as Paul states, the natural creation was "not of its own will . . . subjected to futility" (Rom. 8:20).

Though destined to suffer disruption with and because of humanity's fall, nevertheless the impersonal creation is destined to share the blessings of Christ's redemptive provisions along with redeemed humanity. Paul expresses this ultimate hope of the cosmos as follows:

> The anxious longing of the creation waits eagerly for the revealing of the sons of God. . . . The creation itself also will be set free from its slavery to corruption into the freedom of the glory of the children of God. For we know that the whole creation groans and suffers the pains of childbirth together until now (Rom. 8:19, 21-22).

Certain scholars miss the meaning of Paul's argument entirely when they assign the reference to nature's redemptive hope in Romans 8:19-22 to the as yet unconverted gentile world.[7]

Indeed Peter writes that on the "day of the Lord . . . the heavens will pass away with a roar and the elements will be destroyed with intense heat, and the earth and its works will be burned up" (2 Pet. 3:10-12). However, Peter's statement evidently refers to the renovation by fire of the present natural order, rather than its annihilation. Following this renovation and purification of nature by fire Peter says, "But according to His promise we are looking for new heavens and a new earth, in which righteousness dwells"(2 Pet. 3:13).

Certainly if Paul can say, "Therefore if any man is in Christ, he is a new creature; the old things are passed away; behold, new things have come" (2 Cor. 5:17), it is equally possible for God to make a new natural universe out of the redeemed former one which was corrupted by the Fall. The Bible affords no evidence that God's original creation will ever be annihilated. That it will be redeemed, renovated, purified and changed in form and nature from its present imperfect condition caused by the original Fall is both reasonable and scriptural. Annihilation would indicate an incomplete victory of Christ's redemptive work. Isaiah supports this universal victorious futuristic provision of God's redemptive plan for believing humanity and all nature when he states,

> Also righteousness will be the belt about His loins,
> And faithfulness the belt about His waist. And the
> wolf will dwell with the lamb, And the leopard will
> lie down with the kid, And the calf and the young
> lion and the fatling together; And a little boy will
> lead them. Also the cow and the bear will graze;
> Their young will lie down together; And the lion
> will eat straw like the ox. And the nursing child
> will play by the hole of the cobra, And the weaned

child will put his hand on the viper's den. They will not hurt or destroy in all My holy mountain [kingdom]. For the earth will be full of the knowledge of the Lord As the waters cover the sea. Then it will come about in that day that the nations will resort to the root of Jesse, Who will stand as a signal for the peoples; And His resting place will be glorious. . . . "The wolf and the lamb shall graze together, and the lion shall eat straw like the ox; and dust shall be the serpent's food. They shall do no evil or harm in all my holy mountain," says the Lord (Isa. 11:5-10; 65:25).

Likewise, Paul supports this view in his Ephesian Epistle thus:

He has made known to us his hidden purpose — such was his will and pleasure determined beforehand in Christ — to be put into effect when the time was ripe: *namely, that the universe, all in heaven and on earth, might be brought into a unity in Christ.* In Christ indeed we have been given our share in the heritage, as was decreed in his design whose purpose is everywhere at work. For it was his will that we, who were the first to set our hope on Christ, should cause his glory to be praised. And you too, when you had heard the message of the truth, the good news of your salvation, and had believed it, became incorporate in Christ and received the seal of the promised Holy Spirit; and that Spirit is the pledge that we shall enter upon our heritage, when God has redeemed what is his own, to his praise and glory (Eph. 1:9-14 NEB).

God did not create anything for ultimate annihilation. He created the entire universe to endure forever, whether for weal or woe. The psalmist declared of God, "Thy Kingdom is an everlasting kingdom [Lit., a kingdom of all ages]" (Ps. 145:13; cf. Pss. 10:16; 29:10; 2 Pet. 1:11). Again the psalmist declared: "Indeed, the world is firmly established, it will not be moved. . . .

Thy testimonies are fully confirmed, O Lord, for ever-more" (Ps. 93:1, 5). One has remarked on verse 5 of this psalm that "the final verse is a comment by the psalmist upon the impregnable structure of God's kingdom. His unchangeableness is rooted in His own holiness and in His righteous administration of all creation."[8] Another notes on Psalm 93:1:

> That the earth should be solidly seated in its hidden foundation, is itself a marvel, but this wonder is mentioned only to bring into greater relief the thought . . . that the throne of God, to which the earth is only a footstool, has its foundation firm and everlasting, free from the vicissitudes which beset earthly monarchies.[9]

Yet another remarks: "The consequence of his [God's] victorious rule is that 'the world is established' immovably and his 'throne is established from of old.' "[10]

Adam Clarke states on the words "The Lord reigneth" (Ps. 93:1), "Nature is his agent: or rather, nature is the sum of the laws of his government; the operations carried on by the Divine energy, and the effects resulting from those operations."[11]

On the everlastingness of God's creation Wesley says, "He will overrule all the confusions in the world, so that they shall end in the erection of that kingdom of the Messiah, which can never be moved."[12]

After his interpretation to King Nebuchadnezzar of what was to follow his kingdom in a succession of great temporal dominions, Daniel concludes that array of earthly political power and magnificence, each of which ends in utter failure, with a delineation of God's restored everlasting kingdom (Dan. 2:28-43). Daniel states:

> And in the days of those kings the God of heaven will set up a kingdom which will never be destroyed, and that kingdom will not be left for another people; it will crush and put an end to

all these kingdoms, but it will itself endure forever (Dan. 2:44).

This everlasting kingdom of which Daniel spoke was to be the kingdom of the Messiah, Jesus Christ. This is to be the end product of His redemptive work in which God's entire creation, with the exception of unbelieving and rebellious humanity, will be restored to its original perfection and everlasting divine purpose. Would-be world rulers and their dominions rise, flourish, and fall into oblivion, but the Creator and His creation will outlast the temporal ages and endure forever.

In the light of God's original commission given to humanity to "subdue and have dominion" over the created order (Gen. 1:28 KJV), it is reasonable to suppose that all of humanity's God-approved achievements throughout history will be restored in a purified and perfected state in Christ's future kingdom. All the *cultural* and *scientific values* achieved by men throughout history will be redeemed and serve in Christ's ongoing kingdom in the future restoration. Nothing of real value will ever be lost from history. *Only the disvalues will perish.*

None of this argument against ultimate annihilation is intended to deny the continuous process of change in nature. That all of nature undergoes a process of recycling has been recognized throughout the ages, and such is universally recognized by science to the present. But the conversion of elements from one form into another does not mean the loss of those elements. They simply take new and different forms. Even John Wesley is reported to have said that he expected to see his favorite horse in the future life, though this may have been said with tongue in cheek.

Richard Lovelace states on this issue;

There are still futurologists who are technological optimists. The most notable of these is probably inventor and author R. Buckminster Fuller. His optimism is based on a denial of the Second Law of Thermodynamics or entropy. That law teaches that everything in the universe is running down like an unwinding piece of clockwork. Fuller believes that life and knowledge are anti-entropic, and that humanity will survive [in this temporal age] by what he calls, "ephemeralization" — doing more and more with less and less . . . . From that we should move into a post industrial society based on moral, intellectual, cultural, and spiritual growth.[13]

The Concept of Death in Relation to Humanity

It is both interesting and inspiring to note that throughout the Gospels the death of Jesus Christ is almost, if not always, directly or indirectly associated with His resurrection. The apostles also maintain this association (cf. 1 Cor. 15:3ff.; Rom. 1:4). Peter, quoting from David in Psalm 16:8-11, takes note of the Messiah's forthcoming victory over death: "MOREOVER MY FLESH ALSO WILL ABIDE IN HOPE; BECAUSE THOU WILT NOT ABANDON MY SOUL TO HADES [the grave], NOR ALLOW THY HOLY ONE TO UNDERGO DECAY" (Acts 2:26-27).

When Paul speaks of the believer's death with Christ he refers to his transfer from the state of condemnation unto death under the moral law to a new spiritual life and freedom in Christ — from the law of death to the law of life in Christ (Gal. 5:1; 6:14, cf. 1 John 3:1).

Paul makes clear that Christ's victory over death is efficacious only for those who believe in Him and His redemptive work, and not for the unbeliever. Phillips renders Paul's words in this respect most graphically thus:

We Christians have the unmistakable "scent" of Christ, discernible alike to those who are being saved and to those who are heading for death. To the latter it seems like the very smell of doom; to the former it has the fresh fragrance of life itself (2 Cor. 2:15-16).

This does not mean, however, that the believer will escape the transition of physical death; but, as stated by Paul, for the believer in Christ the final reality of death is abrogated by Christ's victory over death through His resurrection – "Death is swallowed up in [Christ's resurrection] victory" (1 Cor. 15:54). For the believer death has lost its lethal sting, but for the unbeliever "The sting of death is sin" (1 Cor. 15:56), and from this destiny the Bible offers no hope outside of Christ. The author of the Letter to the Hebrews depicts the pitiable plight of "those who lived their whole lives a prey to the fear of death" (Heb. 2:15 *Phillips*).

If the Second Law of Thermodynamics were taken seriously there are certain respects in which humanity is in the process of dying from birth to the grave. Physiology teaches that the chemical elements of the human body undergo a complete change about every seven years, more or less. The human body itself is never in a static state. The Apostle Paul recognized the impermanence of our physical beings when he said, in the graphic translation of J. B. Phillips,

> We know . . . that if our earthly dwelling were taken down [dissolved], like a tent, we have a permanent house in Heaven, made, not by man, but by God. In the present frame [physical body] we sigh with deep longing for the heavenly house, for we do not want to face utter nakedness when death destroys our present dwelling – these bodies of ours. . . . We want our transitory life to be absorbed into the life that is eternal (2 Cor. 5:1-4).

This, of course, expresses the attitude of the Christian believer, and not that of the unbeliever, toward the dissolution of the physical body in hope of one that cannot be dissolved by time or death.

All our efforts to euphemize death cannot eliminate its occurrence. To say that one has *passed away* still means he died. A *funeral parlor* is still the house of mourning for the dead. *A Garden of Memories* is still the burying place of the dead; and a *mausoleum* still contains the physical remains of the dead. To say that the person was *interred* still means that his body was buried in the ground. Death may be euphemized, but it cannot be denied. Euphemisms may well meliorate the agonies of earthly separations, but they cannot eliminate the certainty of death.

But again, there are other experiences of death than physical – some even more painful than physical death itself.

For many, social death is an excruciatingly painful ordeal. Paul seems to allude to this experience when he states that "none of us lives to himself alone" (Rom. 14:7 NIV). Indeed, one may experience a comparative existence alone, but such a lonely existence is social death and not life per se. The hermit or the recluse has a kind of lonely existence, but this cannot be designated social life. The prisoner condemned to be executed is placed in his *solitary cell on Death Row.*

Many unfortunates exist in the isolation of social death in their confinement in mental and criminal institutions. Likewise, of every two or three marriages in America today, begun in blissful happiness and promise, one ends in divorce – a form of social separation – marital death.

The sentimental love song, "Silver Threads Among the Gold," a favorite of many a few generations ago, well illustrates the effects of matrimonial death. The author wrote those lines out of a sense of deep affection for his wife of many years. Eventually the sharing of the wealth that accrued from the royalties of this popular ballad became an item of contention between the author and his wife. Finally discord resulted in separation. The love relationship that inspired the ballad died in the throes of disagreement and avarice. In the end the wealth was dissipated in the courts and both the author and his wife died in abject poverty in fourth-rate rooming houses in separate cities. In the lifeless hand of each was found a crumpled copy of the song, "Silver Threads Among the Gold." Thus the sin of greed wrought marital death, if not everlasting death, in their lives.

Perhaps one of the saddest of all accounts involving marital death is that of Leo Tolstoy and his wife, as narrated by Dale Carnegie. Tolstoy's fame as an author is well known. It is said that 23,000 books and 56,000 newspaper and magazine articles were written about Tolstoy and that his own writings aggregated 100 volumes.

Carnegie states concerning Tolstoy that "in the early years of his married life he and his wife were so happy that they actually got down on their knees and prayed to Almighty God to continue their heavenly bliss, their divine ecstasy."

Eventually discord, feminine jealousy, and greed on the part of Tolstoy's wife drove them apart and destroyed the mutual love that had earlier cemented their marriage. Carnegie relates further: "Later on they were tragically unhappy. He finally came to loathe the very sight of her, and his dying request was that his wife should not even be permitted to come into his presence."

Tolstoy's life ended in tragedy as a result of his failure in marriage. His wife craved luxury and fame, which Tolstoy came to disdain. She craved riches, but he sought to benefit the poor and underprivileged. Carnegie notes further:

> The Tolstoys were married almost half a century; and sometimes she knelt at his knees and implored him to read to her the exquisite, poignant love passages that he had written about her in his diary forty-eight years previously, when they were both madly in love with each other. As he read of those beautiful happy days that were now gone forever, both of them wept bitterly.

Eventually, at the age of 82 years, Tolstoy could

no longer endure the tragic unhappiness of his home. On October 21, 1910, he ran away from his wife under cover of night, like a fugitive from justice. Eleven days later he died from pneumonia in a lonely railway station, accompanied only by his youngest daughter and a few Russian peasants. Sin had wrought marital death to what was once a lovely marriage relationship.[14]

Perversion of humanity's moral sense is equally evident in the experience and history of mankind. Paul speaks of certain ones, who because of lies and hypocrisy have "their conscience seared [as] with a hot iron" (1 Tim. 4:2 KJV). Phillips translates this as those "whose consciences are as dead as seared flesh," though his statement seems to exceed reality.

Paul's description of the degeneracy and ultimate death dealing sin to humanity's moral conscience, as recorded in Romans 1:18-32, has no equal in sacred or profane literature.

Even Judas, who had experienced the blessings and benefits of three years of fellowship and instruction under the ministry of Jesus Christ, allowed greed for financial gain to pervert his moral conscience to the extent that he could betray and sell his Master for the price of a slave. His own self-destruction in suicide testified to the perversion of his moral conscience.

In secular literature perhaps no one has depicted more vividly the gradual, but ultimate, perversion of conscience than has Edgar Allan Poe in his short stories, "William Wilson" and "The Black Cat." A final note of the doom of conscience rings out in the lines of Poe's "The Raven" in those mournful words, "And my soul from out that shadow that lies floating on the floor/Shall be lifted – nevermore!"[15]

The Impersonal Effects of Death

But death is more than individual or corporate. Nations and empires have risen, prospered, and throbbed with political, economic, social, and cultural vitality.

Babylonia, Egypt, Greece, Rome, Spain, Portugal, France, Italy and Germany have all spread their wings toward world conquest. Each has reached its zenith of power and prosperity and then each has suffered its inevitable internal decay as political rigor mortis has done its deadly work. Today we gaze with wondered amazement at the greatness of these empires that once were, but are no more. Only the ruins remain to witness to the inevitableness of death that works according to the divinely established just laws of nature that humanity cannot defy. Gibbon aptly describes this consequence of the death of a civilization in his famed work *The Decline and Fall of the Roman Empire.* "It is appointed . . . once to die" (Heb. 9:27).

From the humanistic perspective, Bertrand Russell's nihilistic conclusion concerning the future of humanity and the universe itself would appear to be valid, when he writes: "No heroism, no intensity of feeling, can preserve an individual life beyond the grave." Further, Russell's pessimism is expressed when he says that, "The whole temple of man's achievements must inevitably be buried beneath the debris of a universe in ruins. . . ." Any philosophy that rejects this conclusion, Russell asserts, cannot hope to stand. He then concludes that "unyielding despair" is the only firm foundation on which man's future hopes can safely rest.[16]

According to the process of the natural moral law established by God, death is the inevitable and inescapable destiny of humanity and the natural universe.

The Law of Life That Transcends the Law of Death

There is, however, another law operative in the universe — *the law of life* — the supernatural law that transcends the natural moral law of death.

Jesus Christ declared, "I am the resurrection and the life; he who believes in Me shall live even if he dies, and everyone who lives and believes in Me shall never die" (John 11:25-26). "I came that they might have life, and might have it abundantly" (John 10:10). "As sin hath reigned unto death, even so might grace reign through righteousness unto eternal life by Jesus Christ our Lord" (Rom. 5:21 KJV).

In His resurrection Christ conquered death and brought immortality to light (2 Tim. 1:10). If we choose to live by the established natural moral law the die is cast — death is inevitable. If we choose to live by the higher spiritual law, death loses its power and life goes on. Thus Jesus could say, "Whosoever liveth and believeth in me shall never die" (John 11:26 KJV).

God did not create mankind and the universe for ultimate annihilation. He created both for all time. And though death works according to the natural moral law, God has a plan of redemption for humanity and the universe which contravenes the law of sin and death. Through faith in and obedience to God's higher redemptive spiritual law death loses its meaning. When the psalmist said, "Yea though I walk through the valley of *the shadow of death,*" he signified that for the believer only the shadow and not the reality of death remains. Thus he could say, "I shall fear no evil" (Ps. 23:4 KJV).

Indeed, all must pass the way of death (Heb. 9:27). However, it is not so much death that is feared as is dying. For the believer death casts its shadow over the valley to frighten the pilgrim as he passes through that dark valley, but the believer finds his consolation in the fact that for him Christ has passed that way before him, and thus he knows that death for him is but a tunnel and not a tomb — that for him death is not final. It is but a passing event on the way into God's eternal presence. When Christ passed that way before us He removed the sting of death and left it powerless to harm the believing pilgrim (1 Cor. 15:55, 57). For the believer, Christ left only the shadow of death. The reality of death that cast that shadow He destroyed through His victorious resurrection from the dead for all believers

(John 11:25-26).

How well David Gregg has expressed this hope and necessity of the continuance of life beyond what men call death, as follows:

"There is a future life for man." It is a necessity. Every faculty of man demands it. His nature was made for it. His soul cries for God, the ever-living God. . . . Above the physical is the mental, seeking if perchance it may find out God; above the mental is the moral, with the index finger pointing to God; above the moral is the spiritual, and that perpetually reaches aloft after God, the ever-living God. For the satisfaction and completion of the upper nature of man eternity is necessary. . . . There was another reason why we concluded that there is a future life for man. It was a reason drawn from God. It was this: the reputation, character, credit of God as a perfect worker, demand a life beyond this life. . . . Human love was made for eternity. Contrast human love with animal love and you will see this. The animal mother loves her offspring until it is able to take care of itself, and then that natural affection ceases. Not so with the love of the human mother. She may be bent with the weight of fourscore years and ten, and her living son may be more than threescore years, but yet that first natural love, instead of ceasing, is seemingly growing stronger, and is just as heartily reciprocated. . . . Does this love continue that it may be disappointed? This testimony of love is a great thing. It is nature's true index pointing to a reunion in the world of spirits. This love for the friends who have gone, and our faith in a future life, match each other, fit each other, and are two halves of a corresponding whole.[17]

This has been so well expressed by the American Quaker poet, Whittier:

Alas for him who never sees
The stars shine through his cypress-trees!

> Who, hopeless, lays his dead away,
> Nor looks to see the breaking day
> Across the mournful marbles play!
> Who hath not learned in hours of faith,
>   The truth to flesh and sense unknown,
> That Life is ever lord of Death,
>   And Love can never lose its own.[18]

End Notes

CHAPTER I

[1]David Elton Trueblood, *Philosophy of Religion* (Grand Rapids: Baker Book House, 1975), p. 212.

[2]W. Schmithals, "Death," *The New International Dictionary of New Testament Theology,* Colin Brown, Gen. Ed. (Grand Rapids: Zondervan, 1975), 1:430.

[3]Ibid, 1:431.

[4]Frederick D. Kershner, *Horizons of Immortality* (St. Louis: Bethany Press, 1926), p. 115.

[5]Ibid.

[6]The foregoing discussion concerning Enoch is taken in the main from *The Wesleyan Bible Commentary,* Vol. 6, on "Hebrews," by Chas. W. Carter (Grand Rapids: Baker Book House, 1966), pp. 143-144.

[7]Adam Clarke, *Clarke's Commentary* (Nashville: Abington-Cokesbury, n.d.), 6:98-99.

[8]Leslie S. McCaw, F. Davidson, Ed., *The New Bible Commentary* (Grand Rapids: Eerdmans, 1954), p. 479.

[9]Archdeacon Aglen, Charles John Ellicott, Ed., *Ellicott's Commentary on the Whole Bible* (Grand Rapids: Zondervan, rep., n.d.), 4:226.

[10]George Arthur Buttrick, *The Interpreter's Bible* (New York–Nashville: Abingdon, 1955), 4:504.

[11]Clarke, *Clarke's Commentary,* 3:516-517.

[12]John Wesley, *Explanatory Notes Upon the Old Testament* (Salem, Ohio; Schmul Publishers, rep. 1975), 3:1762.

[13]Richard Lovelace, V. Gilbert Beers, Ed., *Christianity Today* (Carol Stream, IL, August 5, 1983), p. 13.

[14]The foregoing account has been gleaned from Dale Carnegie's *Five Minute Biographies* (New York: Permabooks, 1949), pp. 57-60.

[15]Edgar Allan Poe, "The Raven," *One Hundred and One Famous Poems* (Chicago: The Cable Company, 1929), pp. 115-119.

[16]Bertrand Russell, *Selected Papers of Bertrand Russell* (New York: Random House, The Modern Library, 1927), pp. 1-3. Quoted by George Forell in *The Protestant Faith* (Philadelphia: Fortress Press, 1975), pp. 145-146.

[17]David Gregg, *The Heaven Life, or Stimulus for Two Worlds* (New York: Revell, 1895), pp. 45-47, 49-51.

[18]John Greenleaf Whittier (1807-1892). *The Complete Poetical Works of John Greenleaf Whittier.* (Boston: Houghton, Mifflin & Co., 1884).

Chapter II
Personal Existence After Physical Death

The Reality of the Second Death

The Bible clearly speaks of a "second death" (Rev. 20:6, 14; 21:8), but the second is the final confirmation of the first – the divine pronouncement of finality – the ultimate closing of the prison gate of solitary confinement to which the condemned prisoner is everlastingly consigned.

The *second death* is a term applied only to unbelievers who die in their sins in divorcement from God. For those who die in the Lord, the Bible declares that "God shall wipe away all tears from their eyes; and *there shall be no more death,* neither sorrow, nor crying, neither shall there be any more pain: for the former things are passed away" (Rev. 21:4 KJV).

Only in the book of Revelation is the *second death* specifically spoken of, though it is implicit elsewhere in the New Testament. It is first stated in Revelation by implication as the ultimate experience of those who fail to overcome the first death through saving faith in Christ: "He who overcomes shall not be hurt by the second death" (Rev. 2:11; cf. Rev. 20:6, 14; 21:8, mar. NASB). And by implication the revelator attributes the second death to those who, because they died outside of Christ's mercy, will have no part in the first resurrection (Rev. 20:5-6).

Again the revelator characterizes the second death as a lake of fire into which the unbelieving immoral will enter following their first death. "But for the cowardly and unbelieving and abominable and murderers and immoral persons and sorcerers and idolators and all liars, their part will be in the lake that burns with fire and brimstone, which is the second death" (Rev. 21:8). Whether one wishes to regard this description in a figurative or literal sense, the conditions that characterize the doomed and their hopeless state remain quite the same. Reflection upon the oil-covered flaming waters of Pearl Harbor where some two thousand American servicemen were burned alive when the Japanese bombed their ships on December 7, 1941, makes the horrors of those who experience this second death the more realistic.

Nowhere is the finality of the second death more explicitly stated than in connection with the final judgment. Those who died without their names inscribed in the Book of Life when they experienced the first death will enter the world of hopeless doom: "This is the second death" (Rev. 20:14; cf. Luke 16:19-31).

The Finality of the Lost Soul's Death[1]

No more solemn words are found in sacred or secular literature than those written of the doomed soul described by Christ in the Gospel of Luke: "In hell he lift up his eyes, being in torments" (Luke 16:23 KJV), or "In hell, where he was in torment, he looked up" (NIV).

The mention of this presently much neglected Bible doctrine at once raises three relevant questions: namely, (1) What is the origin of the doctrine of hell? (2) What is the nature of hell? and (3) What is the significance of hell? It is the author's purpose to answer in part these three questions.

The Origin and Development of the Doctrine of Hell

The twin convictions of the justice of God based upon His absolute righteousness, and the ethical nature of man reflecting on that divine righteousness and justice, are the golden threads that bind together the biblical doctrine of redemption. Inherent in human nature from the beginning was the ethical sense of equity. Equity demands reparation for wanton wrongs and divine approval for benevolent acts. Upon this basis rests all moral justice. At no time in their history was the thinking of the Hebrews an exception to this rule. That God rewards the good and punishes the evil is of the very essence of Hebrew moral theology.

For a time early Hebrew thought appears to have so interpreted the idea that God visits "the iniquity of the fathers on the children, on the third and the fourth generations of those who hate Me" (Exod. 20:5) in such a way as to make the clan responsible for the evil of its individual members. In this interpretation their sense of moral justice found a measure of satisfaction in corporate retribution, either in the present or the future life. The rabbis, however, interpreted the words "of those who hate Me" (Exod. 20:5) to imply individual responsibility. Indeed the Deuteronomic law made specific the individual, as opposed to the corporate, responsible for evil (see Deut. 24:16). Jeremiah and Ezekiel likewise refuted the earlier interpretation of transmitted guilt for evil with the consequent punishment of posterity, and made clear the doctrine of personal responsibility as the determinant of divine retribution (see Jer. 31:29-30; Ezek. 18:14). However, with Ezekiel, God's mercy often transcended His justice, and consequently His long-suffering did not always demand immediate punishment in the death of the sinner.

Ezekiel comes nearer to the idea of a life beyond the present where retribution will be realized, if indeed he does not arrive at that idea. John Clarke Archer may go too far when he states that "hereafter and judgment merging into immortality are always included in Hebrew theology. In fact any idea of final termination – whether by loss of identity or annihilation appears always to have been abhorrent to the Hebrew thinkers."[2] Certainly there has always existed in humanity a sense, implicit if not explicit, that the present life is not the whole of existence. Nevertheless, there seems to be but little light shed on the future life in the Old Testament. Any attempt to attribute this future notion of rewards and retribution to Zoroastrian influence upon the Hebrews' theology is totally unsatisfactory, when all the relevant factors are duly considered.

It should be noted that the Zoroastrian religion did not arise earlier than the sixth century B.C. By this time the Hebrew religion was most likely upward of 1,000 years old from the giving of the Law on Sinai, if the earlier date of Moses' reception of the Law is accepted. It is not likely that the Hebrew theology should have been influenced by the fledgling Zoroastrian religion at that late date.

Man, in the Hebrew view, consisted of two essential parts: namely, flesh (*basar*) and breath (*nefesh*). At death the flesh returned to dust, but the breath persisted as a disembodied spirit. This spirit was thought to retain many of its former powers, and also to have gained some new ones, especially greater freedom and knowledge. However, the idea of a community of spirits, and possibly some faint conception of bodies, seems to have persisted in Hebrew thought. During patriarchal times we read of men who at death were "gathered unto their fathers" (see Gen. 15:15; 25:8, 17; 49:33). Thus this future existence seemed to provide for an opportunity to realize justice, even if corporate rather than individual.

Further, it seemed logical to the Hebrews that the soul and body in substantial union committing good and evil in the present life should justly receive in common their rewards or retribution in the life to come. To them this view was more acceptable than that the soul alone should partake of eternal bliss or woe, as the Greeks taught, and thus they came near to the concept of a bodily resurrection, even for the wicked.

Here the question may be fairly raised as to whether the doctrine of hell formed any part of the divine revelation given by God to Moses in the law. It would seem from a careful examination of the Scriptures that this doctrine was implicit rather than explicit in the Old Testament revelation. In fact James Orr states that "such conceptions . . . did not rest on revelation, but were rather the natural ideas formed of the future state, in contrast with life in the body, in the absence of revelation."[3] However, the same authority declares that "retribution for sin is a cardinal point in the teaching of both the Old Testament and the New Testament."[4] Thus, whether implicit or explicit, the Hebrews' moral demand for justice, unrealized in the present life, found a degree of satisfaction in their belief in divine retribution in the life beyond the grave.

The apocryphal literature makes much of the doctrine of hell, as also of a sort of purgatory, especially as taught by the school of Shammai during the intertestamental period. It was during this time that the doctrine of hell came to its fullest development prior to the New Testament era. By the advent of the New Testament era the doctrine was fully embedded in the orthodox Pharisaic theology, although it was rejected by the more liberal Sadducees. Both John the Baptist and Jesus Christ explicitly and emphatically preached a doctrine of hell that accorded with the doctrine as it was then expressed in Jewish theology. Thus Christ's use of the doctrine, as found in the Gospels, especially in Luke 16, is certainly adequate to validate it as being of divine origin. While the doctrine of hell is mainly implicit in John's Gospel and the Epistles, it is explicit in the synoptic Gospels and Revelation.

The Nature of Hell

The nature of hell seems to have been represented most fully by certain Old Testament figures of speech which were designed to describe the abode of the wicked dead: namely, *Sheol, Gehenna,* and *The Pit.*

James Orr held that while *Sheol* originally signified the abode of the dead in general, it eventually came to mean "almost exclusively the place of the punishment of the lost or finally impenitent; the place of torment of the wicked."[5] "*Sheol* is regarded," says R. H. Charles, "as the place of final eternal punishment, that is, it has become hell."[6] In Luke 16:19-31 the equivalent Greek word *Hades* is used in the foregoing sense (cf. Pss. 49:14-15; 73:18-20).

Gehenna, according to Tischendorf and certain other scholars, is derived through the Aramaic from the Hebrew expression, "Valley of Hinnom." Hinnom was variously known as "The Valley," "The Accursed Valley," and "The Deep Valley" (see Josh. 15:8, 18:16; 2 Kings 23:10; 2 Chron. 26:9; 28:3; 33:6; Neh. 2:13, 15; 3:13; 11:30; Jer. 7:31-32; 19:2, 6). This valley lay to the south-southwest of Jerusalem. The word *Gehenna* appears to have been used in the topographical sense, the religious sense signifying the location of idolatrous nonhuman sacrifice, and as a place of punishment for rebellious or apostate Jews before the righteous.

Finally, *The Pit* appears to have signified the intermediate place of punishment of guilty angels and kings. All three of these ideas are carried over into the New Testament and incorporated into the doctrine of hell as taught by Christ and His apostles. Human suffering, as a consequent of and the just compensation for unrepented evil committed in the present life, is clearly the

Bible teaching concerning the nature of hell (Rom. 6:23).

Hell in its real essence is spiritual. Whatever the implications of the physical figures used in describing the horrors of hell, it finally resolves itself into a spiritual experience that is more awfully real than any physical suffering. Maurice has well said that "the eternal [everlasting] punishment is the punishment of being without the knowledge of God, who is love, and Jesus Christ who has manifested it; even as eternal life is declared to be the having the knowledge of God and of Jesus Christ."[7] The ultimate and awful result of sin is the complete loss of the life and love of God from the soul of man.

That hell, by its very nature, is the everlasting conscious suffering of the lost soul, is the clear teaching of the Scriptures. Nowhere is the word *everlasting*, when used of hell, given the slightest hint of temporal limitation. It appears evident that no other reasonable exegesis of the word can be given than the full sense of endlessness (see Matt. 18:8; 25:41, 46; 2 Thess. 1:9; Jude 7; Rev. 14:11; 19:3; 20:10).

Consciousness, as opposed to "soul sleep" or the "annihilation of the wicked," is clearly implied in the Scriptures, and is requisite to the idea of suffering in hell. This is made doubly clear in the account of the rich-poor man in hell, as recorded in Luke 16:19-31.

The Significance of Hell

The real significance of hell is the soul's awful consciousness of its lostness — its total loss of contact with God. That there are degrees of lostness in the present life is evident, but that there is also the possibility of an ultimate total loss of God from the spiritual consciousness of man is equally real. Such a condition is hell! It is a hell that many have initially experienced in the present life, some even to the dethronement of reason. But it is a hell that will haunt the mind of man who is ultimately lost through endless millennia in the world to come. Then lost man will be utterly alone with no voice to be heard except the echo of his own wail of woe, and no familiar landmark to establish his sense of personal identity or give him direction. Whatever the biblical figures employed to describe the horrors of hell may be, the real meaning is utter lostness, expressed by Christ as "outer darkness" (Matt. 25:30).

Again the meaning of hell is ultimate and utter hopelessness. The soul that is lost in hell will be so by reason of the willful rejection of God's provision of salvation in Christ Jesus. Thus man in hell will have terminated there against God's will and at the expense of having taken himself beyond God's reach. Hell is "outer darkness." "God is light, and in Him there is no darkness at all" (1 John 1:5). Therefore hell is outside of and beyond the presence and reach of God. If man would, he could not save himself, nor can God save him from the hell that is beyond this life and outside of God, for the finally impenitent. If man *will not* be saved in this life, he *cannot* be saved in the life to come. One has significantly queried, concerning the effects of hell on character: "Like the photographer's chemical bath, may its effects not be to develop and fix existing character, rather than to change it?"[8] With the Apostle Paul, in faith we "wait for His Son from heaven, whom He raised from the dead, that is Jesus, who delivers us from the wrath to come" (1 Thess. 1:10).

It is as much the moral responsibility of the Christian minister to declare the awful and solemn truth of the scriptural doctrine of hell, from which Christ died to deliver man, as it is his moral duty to declare the glorious truth of God's love and mercy expressed in Christ's redemptive work on the cross (cf. 1 Thess. 1:10). Redemption takes its meaning from its power to deliver man from the ultimate consequence of sin, the awful ultimate state of the lost, which is hell!

However, it should be noted that the ideas of immortality or everlasting life, and of everlasting existence, are to be sharply distinguished one from the other. Immortality belongs to the redeemed only, as it consists of the life of God (Gk., *zoe*) imparted to the believer at the moment of his conversion to Christ. Jesus said: "I give eternal life to them" (John 10:28; cf. Rom. 6:23). And Paul wrote to Timothy that Christ "alone possesses immortality" or God only is the source of immortality (1 Tim. 6:16). Certainly the lost will have everlasting existence in the future state, but they will not have immortality, for that belongs to God and those to whom He imparts it through Christ in their salvation.

The Intermediary State

Existence between physical death and the future life is one of the most difficult problems that faces Christian theology. That is commonly known as The Intermediate State. Where do the souls of the deceased go immediately following physical death? What happens to personal consciousness following physical death? These and other related questions have been variously addressed by religious philosophers and theologians. Does the Bible have a satisfactory answer to these questions?

Certain non-Christian speculations will be considered first, after which the biblical pronouncements will be given.

The Doctrines of Universalism and a Second Chance

Basically these doctrines simply mean that all people will eventually be saved, or at least have a second chance. These doctrines, however, are expressed in a variety of ways.

The second-chance view teaches that there will be a second opportunity in the hereafter for those to be saved who died as unbelievers. In the early history of Christianity Origen (185?-?254), and a limited number of Christians, seem to have held this view. Loraine

Boettner notes that the view was also taught by the Anabaptists during the Reformation period, and that in the nineteenth century Schleiermacher (1768-1834) and certain other German and English liberal theologians advocated this view.[9]

Likewise both the Mormons (Latter Day Saints) and the Jehovah's Witnesses (Russellites) have in more recent times taught the second-chance doctrine of salvation.

The Scottish scholar, William Barclay, taught a special brand of universal salvation that approximates the Roman Catholic doctrine of purgatory in certain respects. While Barclay did not deny the doctrine of hell, like Origen he regarded it as punitive correction for those who die without saving faith in Christ. Under the duress of suffering in hell all will, he thought, eventually be won through divine love to ultimate salvation — a sort of unorthodox Protestant purgatory. Barclay says, "I am a convinced universalist. I believe that in the end all men will be gathered into the love of God."[10] And again he says, "If one man remains outside the love of God at the end of time, it means that that one man has defeated the love of God — and that is impossible."[11]

Although Barclay's position is a rather unique brand of universalism, it is typical of this doctrine in that all people will eventually be saved. In certain respects other universalists differ in their speculations. This doctrine, whether taught as a complete denial of hell as the ultimate doom of the unbeliever, or as a "second-chance salvation" after death, is a form of humanism that has no valid basis in Scripture or sound reasoning.

Some mistakenly interpret 1 Peter 3:18-20 to support their views of a second-chance salvation. Admittedly, this is one of the most difficult passages in the Bible to interpret. Charles S. Ball cites a variety of interpretations given on this passage by different scholars.[12]

In consideration of Peter's reference to "the days

of Noah" (v. 20), in which the discussion has its setting, John Wesley's explanation seems the most satisfactory. Wesley states on 1 Peter 3:19-21 the following:

> *By which Spirit he preached* – Through the ministry of Noah. To the spirits in prison – The unholy men before the Flood, who were then reserved by the justice of God, as in prison, till He executed the sentence upon them all: and are now also reserved to the judgment of the great day. *When the longsuffering of God waited* – For a hundred and twenty years; all the time *the ark was preparing* during which Noah warned them all to flee from the wrath to come. *The antitype whereof* – The thing typified by the ark, even *baptism,* now *saveth us* – That is, through the water of baptism we are saved from the sin which overwhelms the world as a flood: not, indeed, the bare outward sign [water baptism], but the inward grace; a divine consciousness that both our persons and our actions are accepted through Him who died and rose again for us.[13]

With Wesley's interpretation Adam Clarke is in essential agreement in his understanding of this difficult passage. In any event the passage lends no support to a second-chance salvation.

Whatever may have been the hope of those who died before Christ provided universal atonement on the Cross, the Scripture makes clear the finality of the lostness of those who die in unbelief. Doubtless the clearest passage in the Bible on this issue is Luke 16:19-31 where Abraham declares to the lost person in the world of doom, "between us and you there is a great chasm fixed, in order that those who wish to come over from here to you may not be able, and that none may cross over from there to us" (v. 26).

The grave dangers of universalism and the second-chance doctrines are severalfold. Among these dangers is the tendency to postpone repentance for sin and submission to Christ during the uncertainties of the present life. They also stultify missionary interest and zeal for the conversion of a world without Christ (see Matt. 28:18-20; Acts 1:8; see also Matt. 13:42; 22:13; 24:51; 25:30; John 8:24; 2 Cor. 5:10; 6:2; Heb. 9:27). And they are contrary to the entire tenor of the biblical teachings concerning the afterlife.

The Doctrine of Soul Sleep

Concisely this doctrine teaches that following physical death the soul or spiritual personality of a person loses all consciousness until the resurrection.

Whether with the body in the grave or in a neutral silent state, the souls of the deceased have no knowledge, consciousness, or activity from the time of death until the resurrection. In fact the spiritual person is non-existent during this time. It is here that this doctrine completely loses its validity. If in this intermediate state the spiritual personality (the conscious person) is non-existent then obviously it is not resurrected, since there would be nothing to resurrect. Thus the so-called resurrection would be an independent creation that would have no continuity with the previous person.

Both the Jehovah's Witnesses and the Seventh Day Adventists have held the "soul sleeping" doctrine as one of their main tenets. Very few others in church history have taught the soul sleep doctrine. It has been consistently rejected by the main body of Christianity throughout church history.

Indeed, the New Testament uses the expression *sleep* in relation to death. Christ said on the occasion of Lazarus' death, "Our friend Lazarus has fallen asleep; but I go, that I may awaken him out of sleep" (John 11:11; cf. Matt. 9:24; Acts 7:60; 1 Cor. 15:15-18; 1 Thess. 4:13-14). However, this expression of *sleep* is used metaphorically in the Scriptures for death, rather than literally. It is spoken of the body rather than the conscious spiritual person. Likewise Jesus' description of the lost man in the afterlife, as given in Luke 16:19-31, completely denies this doctrine. It is not sufficient, as some dubiously hold, that Luke 16:19-31 is a parable and thus does not teach reality. It is the clear teaching of Jesus, and if it is history, as appears most likely, it is the experience of what had happened. If it were a parable, it is still a clear teaching of what may be. Thus the teaching is the same in either event. This account leaves no ground for the erroneous doctrine of soul sleep for those who die without saving faith in God.

There are other evidences in the Bible that give clear witness that believers also experience conscious existence in relation to God immediately following physical death. To the repentant thief on the cross Jesus said, "Truly I say to you, *today* you shall be with Me in Paradise" (Luke 23:43). Likewise the appearance of Moses and Elijah who spoke with Christ on the occasion of His transfiguration, which was before His death and resurrection, gives clear evidence of their knowledge, consciousness, and activity, though their bodies had been dead for many centuries (cf. Matt. 27:52; Luke 20:37-38). Certainly one of the clearest biblical evidences of the believer's soul passing directly into the presence of Christ at death is that of Stephen, the first Christian martyr. In his hour of death Stephen said, " 'I see the heavens opened up and the Son of Man [Christ] standing at the right hand of God.' . . . And they went on stoning Stephen as he called upon the Lord and said, 'Lord Jesus, receive my spirit!' . . . And having said this, he fell asleep [mar. expired]" (Acts 7:56, 59-60; cf. 2 Cor. 5:1-3, 6, 8; Phil. 1:21-23). The overall witness of the Scriptures testifies to the continued consciousness of the spiritual personalities of those who experience physical death.

The Doctrine of Annihilation, or Ultimate Extinction of the Dead

Basically, annihilation means to reduce something

to nonexistence or cessation of being. As a philosophical view it simply means that the entire universe will end in nothingness. It is the ultimate of stark pessimism which is well expressed by Bertrand Russell, as previously noted. Also the French existential atheist philosopher Jean-Paul Sartre (1905-1982) held this view in a term which he designated *nullity,* or nothingness. Since with Sartre existence precedes essence, all must end ultimately in nullity. Having begun with nothing all must end in nothing — *ex nihilo nihil fit.*

Theologically this view is usually applied to the unbelievers at death, or in certain instances to those unbelievers who have experienced a second chance after death and have rejected that offer of salvation.

Both Seventh Day Adventists and Jehovah's Witnesses have been ardent advocates of this view. Whether at death, after rejecting a second offer of salvation following death or, as held by some, at the final judgment, all unbelievers will be annihilated. The Russellites (Jehovah's Witnesses) often quote that "the wicked will be burned up root and branch" (Mal. 4:1) in support of this doctrine. Boettner explains this doctrine as follows:

> The form in which this view usually has been held is that man was created mortal, and that immortality is a gift which God confers as a reward upon the righteous, although some have held that man was created immortal but that the wicked are, as a positive act of God, deprived of that gift.[14]

The doctrine of annihilation is a rationalistic attempt to escape the consequences of human sin and the misery to which it leads in the future life. It has no support in either reason or the Scriptures. God created nothing for ultimate annihilation — of either nature or persons. Though the Fall and sin have perverted and corrupted God's created order, neither God's will nor sin itself can annihilate what God has created. God has provided universal salvation, and if mankind rejects that plan they will suffer the consequences. It is only as they continue to exist that it is possible for them to suffer those consequences. Such is not an arbitrary divine imposition of the consequences imposed by God upon the unbelievers after death, but rather the result of the course the unbelievers have chosen. They take themselves beyond the reach of God's mercy.

The Bible is clear in its teaching concerning the everlasting existence of the lost:

> Then He will also say to those on His left, "Depart from Me, accursed ones, into the *eternal* fire which has been prepared for the devil and his angels"; . . . and these will go away into eternal punishment, but the righteous into eternal life (Matt. 25:41, 46).[15]

The Spiritualist Cult and Death

The name of this cult is more accurately designated *Spiritism* than *Spiritualism* as it deals with spirits rather than spirituality. This is the oldest and the most degenerate form of all the known cults. Its origin is lost in antiquity. It is found among the ancient Chinese, Hindus, Babylonians, Egyptians, and primitive animistic religions the world over to the present day. It appears in both the Old and the New Testaments, though always under condemnation from God, and remnants are traceable in the Roman Catholic Church. It has usually flourished in times of war and human disasters when people are faced with the mysteries of death.

Historically, Spiritism made its appearance in America at Hydeville, New York, with Margaret and Kate Fox in 1847. The Fox sisters, ages twelve and nine, lived in a supposedly haunted house with their parents where the skeleton of one Charles Rosma, who reportedly had been murdered by a Mr. John Bell, was found in the basement. The Fox sisters reportedly experienced eerie visitations from the ghost of Charles Rosma during the nighttime. They purportedly developed a communication code with the visiting ghost of Charles Rosma by the snapping of their fingers and the cracking of their toes.

Incredible as the foregoing seems, as a result of the Fox sisters' experiences, Spiritist seances spread rapidly and extensively over the United States, and from there to Great Britain and Europe. One authority states that in less than twenty years from its origin the National Spiritualist (or Spiritist) Association was organized in 1863. The same authority states that by 1945 there were 228,000 Spiritists in the United States, and by the same year the British Spiritualist Union had 500 churches and 18,000 members.

This cult is basically pantheistic, or perhaps more accurately designated "pan-psychic monism." All that exists is a universal mind, and all else is simply modes or reflections of that universal mind. This psychic world is the reality of the visible or empirical world, though the former is incomparably more wonderful and beautiful. The afterlife will be spent in seven different spheres or concentric circles, each of which will carry the deceased farther away from the present life into a yet more blissful existence in the outer spheres.

Spiritism functions in a variety of ways. Psychic force is greatly enhanced by group concentration. Central to Spiritism is the *seance.* At the *seance* the *medium* goes into a trance and receives purported messages from the spirits of the departed in one of the seven spheres which the medium then conveys to the *sitters* in the seance. Various phenomena are reported to occur during these seances, among which are noninformational manifestations such as poltergeists.

Among the many modern literary sources of Spiritism are the works of Stewart Edward White, *The Betty Books* (1937), *Across the Unknown* (1939), *The Unobstructed Universe* (1940), the works of A. Conan Doyle, the New Age Movement and the works of Shirley MacLaine, to mention only a few.

Since all is one mind, Spiritists do not believe in either a future heaven or hell. Both heaven and hell are present aspects of the total psychic universe. At death the person simply passes into a progressive graduation of the seven outer spheres.

Perhaps the most noted instance of contemporary Spiritism has been the world-renowned Episcopal Bishop James Pike. From his California Episcopacy he finally resorted to a Spiritist medium in London in an attempt to make contact with his former secretary who had committed suicide, and his son James Pike, Jr., who had shot himself in a New York hotel. He also claimed to have contacted Paul Tillich who had preceded him into the nether world. In August 1969 Pike fell from a cliff in Palestine near the Qumran ruins and was killed.

Among the various occurrences and condemnations of Spiritism in the Bible the best known and best representative is the account of King Saul's visit to the house of the witch of Endor, when in utter despair he faced the powerful army of the Philistines and knew that God had departed from him and the prophet Samuel had died. The account is impressively depicted in the twenty-eighth chapter of First Samuel.

While various interpretations of this incident have been given, the present writer believes the entire incident to have been a psychic episode.

When King Saul resorted to the tent of the witch of Endor the burden of his mind was the prophet Samuel who had previously given him messages and directions from God in times of crises. But Samuel is now dead and the voice of God is silent in the soul of King Saul. He is faced with certain defeat in battle by the Philistine army the next day. In despair he goes to the witch of Endor in anticipation of some message of hope through the prophet Samuel.

Not recognizing the identity of King Saul, the witch of Endor (a Spiritist medium and a highly skilled psychic) read the burdened mind of Saul and there saw the figure of Samuel whom she described to Saul. Recognizing the identity of Samuel as described by the witch and hearing his repeated message of hopelessness, Saul prostrated himself on the floor of the witch's tent in utter despair. The witch, suddenly recognizing the identity of King Saul who had sworn to destroy all the witches from his kingdom, was smitten with fear for her own life.

If witches have power to call the righteous dead out of God's presence then evil is greater than good or God. Furthermore she called the image of Samuel *up* out of the deep of Saul's troubled consciousness, and not out of the dark underworld.[16]

As Browning is understood by the present author, perhaps no one has so graphically depicted this incident of King Saul at the tent of the Witch of Endor that dark and fatal night as has Robert Browning in his description of "the king-serpent" (boa constrictor) in his lines entitled "Saul."

> He stood as erect as that tent-prop, both arms stretched out wide
> On the great cross-support in the center, that goes to each side;
> He relaxed not a muscle, but hung there as, caught in his pangs
> And waiting his change, the king-serpent all heavily hangs,
> Far away from his kind, in the pine, till deliverance come
> With the spring-time, – so agonized Saul, drear and stark, blind and dumb.[17]

Likewise Rudyard Kipling has expressed it well in his lines:

> Oh the road to Endor is the oldest road,
> And the craziest road of all,
> Straight it runs to the witch's abode
> As it did in the days of Saul.

> And nothing has changed of the sorrow in store
> For such as go down on the road to Endor.[18]

Spiritism, ancient or modern, has given no satisfactory answer to the state, abode, or activities of the deceased. That answer is to be found in the Bible only.

End Notes

CHAPTER II

[1]Formerly printed in *The Preacher's Magazine,* June/July/August, 1982, under the title "The Future State of the Lost" (Kansas City, MO: Beacon Hill Press, pp. 38-40). Used by permission.

[2]John Clarke Archer, *Faiths Men Live By* (New York: Thomas Nelson and Sons, 1934), p. 355.

[3]James Orr, *International Standard Bible Encyclopedia,* 4:2761.

[4]Ibid.

[5]Ibid.

[6]R. H. Charles, *Eschatology.* (New York: Schocken Books, 1970), p. 236.

[7]Maurice, Frederick Denison, *Theological Essays,* p. 450.

[8]Orr, *ISBE,* 4:2503.

[9]Loraine Boettner, *Immortality* (Philadelphia: Presbyterian and Reform Publishing Co., 1956), p. 104.

[10]William Barclay, *A Spiritual Autobiography* (Grand Rapids: Eerdmans, 1975), p. 58.

[11]Ibid., p. 60.

[12]See Charles S. Ball, *The Wesleyan Bible Commentary,* 6 vols. (Grand Rapids: Baker Book House, 1966), 6:267, 268.

[13]John Wesley, *Explanatory Notes Upon the New Testament* (London: The Epworth Press, rep. 1954), pp. 882, 883, notes 19-21.

[14]Boettner, *Immortality,* p. 117.

[15]See also Daniel 12:2; Matthew 7:23; Mark 9:43-49; Luke 16:24; 2 Thessalonians 1:9; Jude 7; 13; Revelation 14:11; 20:10.

[16]For other biblical accounts of Spiritism and its condemnation see Genesis 3:1; Deuteronomy 32:17; 1 Kings 22:19-23; 1 Chronicles 10:13; Isaiah 19:3; Ezekiel 28:11-19; Acts 8:9-24; 13:6-11; 16:16-18; 1 Corinthians 10:20; Revelation 12:9.

[17]Roma A. King, Jr., Gen. Ed. *The Complete Works of Robert Browning.* (Athens, Ohio: Ohio University Press, 1973), p. 247.

[18]Rudyard Kipling. Quoted by Boettner in *Immortality,* p. 149.

Chapter III
The Doctrine of Purgatory

Introduction

The official Roman Catholic definition of purgatory is as follows:

> Purgatory . . . is the place and state in which souls suffer for a while and are purged after death, before they go to Heaven, on account of their sins. Venial (q.v.) sins, which have never in life been remitted by an act of repentance or love or by good deeds, and grave sins, the guilt of which is eternal punishment has indeed been removed by God after an act of repentance but for which there is still left a debt of temporal punishment due to his justice on account of the imperfection of that repentance, must be purged away after death by the pain of intense longing for God, whose blissful vision is delayed, and also, as is commonly taught, by some pain of sense, inflicted probably by material fire. It is of faith that those in purgatory can be helped by the prayers and sacrifices of the faithful on earth and especially by the acceptable Sacrifice of the Altar. Though there is no ecclesiastical decision in the matter, it is a common custom to pray *to* the souls in purgatory that they will intercede for us with God.[1]

The relatively recent date of this source (1949 — Rev. Ed.) should reflect the contemporary Catholic theological concept and teaching of the dogma of purgatory. From the foregoing definition it is evident that purgatory belongs to the theological category of soteriology in Roman Catholic doctrine. Certain essential notes of the dogma are presented in this definition which should be observed at the outset.

(1) Purgatory is declared to have both a definite "place," and to be a "state" where the souls of the dead "suffer" "temporarily" for the purging from their sins before entering heaven.

(2) The specified sins for which they suffer are venial (sins that may be pardoned), which were not remitted in life since they were neither repented of nor equated by "love" or by "good deeds," and "grave sins" the guilt and eternal punishment of which God has removed after repentance, but which sins entail "a debt of temporal punishment due to . . . [God's] justice" because of imperfect repentance.

(3) This guilt is declared to be removed in purgatory by "the pain of intense longing for God whose blissful vision is delayed," apparently because of the unpreparedness of an imperfectly purified soul to stand in the presence of the absolutely pure and holy God.

(4) It is assumed by this definition that the essential union of a physical body and a spiritual soul will continue after death in purgatory.

(5) Consequently, physical pain, or "some pain of sense," will be "inflicted probably by material fire."

(6) The prayers and sacrifices of the living, based on the doctrine of the communion of the saints, are assumed by faith to be efficacious for the souls in purgatory, but especially is this true of "the acceptable Sacrifice of the Altar."

(7) Finally, the practice and efficacy of the prayers of those in purgatory for the living is suggested. This last item seems, however, to be in considerable dispute

among Catholic theologians.

Another recent authority observes that certain of the Church Fathers have "timidly" suggested that souls in purgatory may pray for and thus help the living. However, this same authority notes that this is not a commonly accepted doctrine, and that souls in purgatory first need the help of their living brethren to attain to eternal happiness as soon as possible. Then he concludes that the common Catholic doctrine is that the living can help those in purgatory, but that they (those in purgatory) are not yet in a position to help the living by their prayers.[2]

It appears that at best there is confusion and disagreement among Catholic scholars on the question of whether souls in purgatory offer prayers for the living. But this is not the only purgatorial doctrine on which there was evidently disagreement by the close of the Middle Ages. Luther took quite an opposite view on certain other items, which opposing views were condemned in the Bull "Exsurge Domine," June 15, 1520, by Holy Pontiff, based on the Lateran Council V, 1512-1517. Luther's condemned views were that,

> The souls in purgatory are not sure of their salvation, at least not all; nor is it proved by any arguments or by the Scriptures that they are beyond the state of meriting or of increasing in charity.
>
> The souls in purgatory sin without intermission, as long as they seek rest and abhor punishment.
>
> The souls freed from purgatory by the suffrages of the living are less happy than if they had made satisfaction by themselves.[3]

Since, however, these views only serve to reflect the extent to which Luther had been influenced by the Church's traditions, they will best be left there.

However, from the foregoing analysis of the Roman Catholic position it would seem that there is no ground, unless Luther is correct, for the Protestant notion that Catholic purgatory may be a sort of "temporary uncertain waiting room of suffering" from which the souls of the departed may eventually be ushered into either eternal bliss or eternal damnation. The certainty of the ultimate efficacy of purgatorial suffering for the purification and preparation of the soul for the enjoyment of the beautiful vision, together with the anticipatory joy inspired by that prospect, has been vividly described by Saint Catherine of Genoa thus:

> I do not believe it would be possible to find any joy comparable to that of a soul in Purgatory, except the joy of the Blessed in Paradise. For every sight, however little, that can be gained of God exceeds every pain and every joy that man can conceive without it.[4]

Thus, it is clearly evident that purgatory is in no sense punitive, as hell is considered to be, but rather it is preparation for heaven. Purgatory becomes, on this account, not something to be feared or dreaded by the Catholic, but rather an experience to be joyfully anticipated since it leads necessarily and certainly to eternal bliss. It is something like the experience of one to undergo necessary major surgery which he knows will entail temporary pain and suffering, but which offers certain release from the greater sufferings occasioned by a serious malady, and consequent restoration to perfect health and happiness; or perhaps like the sufferings of an expectant mother in childbirth who anticipates joyfully the birth of a new life.

The Purported Ground for the Doctrine of Purgatory
There appear to be three major purported foundation stones upon which the Catholic theologians build the doctrine of purgatory. They are (1) the Canonical Scripture and the Apocrypha; (2) the traditional evidences, and (3) the evidence of contemporary reinterpreted Catholic dogma.

W. E. Garrison, a Protestant theologian, wrote in 1952,

> The idea of purgatory has perhaps as shaky a biblical foundation as any Roman Catholic doctrine that pretends to have any at all, but no other has been a more useful invention as a feature in the total technique of priestly control. When we consider how indispensable purgatory now seems to be in the whole scheme of penance, indulgences, absolution, and the like, it is remarkable that the church got on so long with no definite doctrine on the subject.[5]

Such purported biblical foundations as are now cited by Catholic theologians for purgatory are clearly interpolations from later periods of church history when the doctrine began to take root in the thought and practice of the Church. In a figure, they are the supports placed under the building after it was erected, rather than biblical supports upon which the building was constructed.

There are indeed certain passages in the Inter-Testament Apocryphal Literature that indicate a tendency on the part of the Jews of that period to predicate a kind of mediatorial state faintly corresponding to the later Catholic dogma of purgatory. The apocryphal literature makes much of the idea of hell, as also of a sort of purgatory, especially as taught by the school of Shammai during the Inter-Testament Period. There appears to have been no disposition on the part of biblical nor extra-biblical writers of the New Testament era to formulate a doctrine of purgatory, either from the written Scriptures of the Old or New Testament documents, or from extra-biblical sources.

Indeed, Clement of Alexandria (150?–?220), Garrison thinks, was the first of the Early Church Fathers to think that it was "reasonable that wicked souls should have their sins purged away before entering heaven."[6] Clement's inclination toward purgatorial purification seems to have been in accommodation to his disposition toward universalism. Such a doctrine as universalism, if it recognizes the reality of sin and the holiness of God, obviously necessitates some sort of purgation from evil, either in this life or the next. Since it is obvious that not all die in a state of purity, some provision should of necessity be made for their purification after death. About the only Scripture passage that Clement seemed to base his speculations upon was 1 Corinthians 3:15. When it is noted that Paul is dealing with "divisions" and "party spirits" in the church at Corinth in this chapter, with a view to correcting their temporal and humanistic notions of the church, and church leadership in particular, it becomes evident that the passage in question has no relevance to the future life. The readers were carnal or immature babes who were disposed to empiricism rather than spiritual understanding (see 1 Cor. 3:1-9). Only by considering the passage out of context and perverting its real meaning could Clement or any subsequent interpreter give it purgatorial significance.

Saint Augustine (354-430) likewise conjectured a possible period of purgatorial fire just preceding the final general judgment. However, with Augustine this is nothing more than a conjecture to which neither he nor others of his day appear to have attached any weighty significance.

Gregory the Great (540?–604) seems to have been the first to develop something of a sense of certitude about purgatory. However, he had no stronger support for his conviction than a serious misunderstanding and misinterpretation of Matthew 12:31-32. It is evident that Christ meant no more here than to emphasize the danger of the unforgivableness of blasphemy against the Holy Spirit. To draw the inference from this statement of Christ that sins against the Son may be forgiven "*in the world to come,*" and then make that inference the basis of the whole doctrine of purgatory is certainly very unsound exegesis. In fact it can be no less than eisegesis. However, even Gregory the Great was honest enough not to claim for his inference more than a theoretical idea.

Apart from the foregoing passages there is one statement in Paul's first letter to the Corinthians (15:29) which is alleged by Catholics to lend biblical support to the doctrine of purgatory. However, a proper contextual understanding of this apparently obscure passage lifts it totally out of the realm of purgatorial significance.

Traditional Evidence
for the Doctrine of Purgatory

According to Garrison,[7] for many centuries after these early speculations by Clement, Augustine, and Gregory the Great the doctrine of purgatory remained in obscurity and was conflictingly defined and interpreted. However, threats and fears of purgatorial fire were employed by some of the clergy as an incentive to good works and the gaining of indulgences, even long before it was authorized as a doctrine of the Church.

While Garrison states concerning purgatory that "the Council of Trent [1545-1563] set the seal of authority upon it,"[8] certain Roman Catholic authorities place its doctrinal authorization by the Church at an earlier period.

It is admitted by Catholic scholars that the belief in purgatory developed gradually in the living consciousness of the Church. It is purported to have stemmed from two principles: namely, "from everything in Scripture and Tradition that exalts the demands of divine justice and mentions a purifying fire," and "from the liturgical custom of prayers and suffrage for the dead."[9] Then, states this same authority, "it was not until 1439 that the Council of Florence officially defined its existence on the occasion of the controversies with the Greeks,"[10]

The pronouncement on purgatory at the Council

of Florence states:

> It has . . . defined, that, if those truly penitent
> have departed in the love of God, before they
> have made satisfaction by worthy fruits of penance
> for sins of commission and omission, the souls of
> these are cleansed after death by purgatorial
> punishment; and so that they may be released
> from punishments of this kind, the suffrages of the
> living faithful are of advantage to them, namely,
> the sacrifices of Moses, prayers and almsgiving,
> and other works of piety, which are customarily
> performed by the faithful for other faithful accord-
> ing to the instructions of the Church.[11]

Even by this time, however, the nature of the doctrine of purgatory appears confused and uncertain. The
current conception corresponded to the Latin notion of
redemption with its judicial concepts of debts, satisfactions, and reparations. Thus it confused and muddied
the waters of theological thought concerning purification, improvement, and sanctification which were the
redemptive concepts of the Greeks. While Catholics
held that the Church's faith in purgatory was established
at the Council of Florence, they did not profess to know
the real nature of that which had become a dogma.
The nature of its fire, duration, and specific efficacy all
remained uncertain. Notwithstanding this factor of inde-
terminacy, the Church Fathers of the time sought to
evade the tendency of the faithful to take refuge in the
notion that "the duration of purgatory doesn't matter
to me, since I know I shall ultimately attain eternal
life."[12]

So important did this dogma become that anyone
disposed to contradict it was forthwith anathematized.
In the Canons On Justification, No. 30, it is stated that

> if anyone shall say that after the reception of the
> grace of justification, to every penitent sinner the
> guilt is so remitted and the penalty of eternal
> punishment so blotted out that no penalty of tem-

porary punishment remains to be discharged either in this world or in the world to come in purgatory before the entrance to the kingdom of heaven can be opened: let him be anathema.[13]

At Session XXV (Dec. 3 and 4, 1563) of the Council of Trent, the doctrine of purgatory was declared "instructed by the Holy Spirit," to be "in conformity with the sacred writings and the ancient traditions of the Fathers in sacred councils, and very recently in this ecumenical Synod [Council of Trent]." The Council commanded the bishops to insist that "the sound doctrine of purgatory, which has been transmitted by the holy Fathers and holy Councils, be believed by the faithful of Christ, be maintained, taught, and everywhere preached."[14]

Certainly Trent was overlooking a prevalent effect of the purgatorial doctrine when it admonished the omission of teachings "that savor of filthy lucre." So corrupt were the abuses of this doctrine by the time of the Reformation that Karl Adam records:

> In the prevailing of clerical education, preachers of the indulgences such as the Dominican (Tetzel for instance) eagerly seized on Perandis' pronouncement, so that many preachers really did adopt as their favorite tag "your cash no sooner clinks in the bowl than out of purgatory jumps the soul."[15]

Adam fairly admits that "some of the papal decrees themselves were in great measure responsible for this crude interpretation of indulgences."[16]

Nature and Purpose of the Doctrine of Purgatory

It must be noted that the doctrine of purgatory is inextricably bound up with the Roman Catholic concepts of sin and salvation. These concepts are in turn inseparably linked with medieval anthropological notions. Therefore, it is necessary to begin with the nature of man, and work out through the Fall to the nature of sin, and thence to the idea of salvation and its relation to purgatory.

While there is a sense in which a dualistic view of man prevailed in early Christian and Medieval times, at the same time there had developed in Christian thought through the Middle Ages the idea of the "essential union" of body and soul. This becomes explicit in the thought of Thomas Aquinas. Such a concept made the Fall total, in the sense that man's total being, body and soul, participated in the sin that separated him from God. Consequently his total being suffered the results of sin, and his total being stood in need of redemption.

In addition to its implications for the whole cult of Mariolatry, this anthropological concept gave support to the view that sin was somehow related to matter as well as to spirit. To what extent, if any, Neoplatonism contributed to this view must be judged by the reader. All of this in turn gave rise to the practice of asceticism, the monastery, the nunnery, celibacy in the priesthood and even purgatory, as contributing factors to man's total salvation. The sufferings imposed upon the present life, through asceticism, were considered inadequate reparations for the sin that had sent its roots to the very depth of man's nature and bore its evil fruits in every part of his being.

The foregoing Catholic concept of the Fall appears to have regarded human depravity as "extensively total," but not "intensively" so. Therefore, while sin had pervaded the entirety of his being, it had not totally destroyed his moral nature. Consequently, man was not only responsible for the misuse of his God-given freedom in the Fall, but he was also responsible for the employment or appropriation of the God-ordained means for his salvation.

This somewhat dualistic, and at the same time "essentially united," view of sinful man quite naturally led to the view of the forgiveness of sins as relates to the spiritual-moral aspect of sin, but since "sin in the flesh" could not be removed by forgiveness, it was left to be rooted out by suffering. Consequently the notion developed that the sinner could be forgiven of the guilt of overt sin, but he must be purified or sanctified from the consequences of his sinful acts, as also from the sinful nature of the "flesh."

Five factors contributed to the problem. The *first* stemmed from the concept of the "essential union" of body and soul which somehow made the physical body a moral participant in sin with somewhat equal moral responsibility for the results of sin.

The *second* problem stemmed from the correct notion of the absolutely holy and perfect character of God who could not look with favor upon an imperfectly redeemed and restored creature, thus demanding perfect holiness in man.

The *third* problem stemmed from a partial and inadequate view of Christ's atonement as a remedy for the totality of human sin.

The *fourth* problem that contributed to the notion of purgatory as a means of ultimate salvation was the humanistic view of man. This view regarded him as capable, in part at least, of doing for himself what Christ's atonement could not do for him, namely, saving him from the consequences of his forgiven sins and the sin of his flesh through human suffering, which for its completion necessarily extended into an existence after death. This view made a heavy contribution to the Roman Catholic notion of asceticism and purgatory.

The *fifth* factor that contributed to the ideas of asceticism and purgatory was the "equity notion of divine justice," in which God's justice as expressed against sin placed man in His debt. Consequently that debt could be satisfied only by an equal balance of human suffering through penance. It is, of course, evident that this last view is closely related to the inadequate view of Christ's atonement as a complete satisfaction before God for man's sin (cf. Isa. 53:11).

To sum up the foregoing contributing factors, the total physico-spiritual being of man participated in the Fall and suffered the moral consequences. The absolutely holy nature of God required perfect holiness in man. The atonement of Christ provided for man's forgiveness, but not for his cleansing from sin. Man was regarded as capable of and responsible for the completion of his own salvation through human suffering. And finally, God's equitable justice required man to balance accounts of his debt of sin by sufferings in this life and the next. On this reasoning, consciously or inadvertently, the Catholic dogmas of asceticism and purgatory largely developed.

Further, to a more adequate understanding of purgatory, it is necessary to note the Catholic concept of sin.

As viewed by the Roman Church, overt sin is of two types: namely, "mortal" and "venial." Mortal sin is of such a nature, writes one Catholic authority, that

> it entails the death of the soul and is rewarded by an eternal punishment: venial sin is rewarded by a temporal punishment . . . mortal sin attacks the very principle of supernatural life, which is union with God through charity [love].[17]

It is further observed that "through mortal sin the will renounces God and puts its last end in a creature."[18] It appears that certain sins are mortal by reason of the objects they have in view. Some objects are totally incompatible with a final inclination toward God and thus direct the soul ultimately and forever away from God.

It seems that mortal sin may also occur even when the "object" is not of itself foreign to God, if that object excludes charity and is regarded as an end in itself. This Roman Catholic view comes close to Paul Tillich's notion of idolatry as the result of making anything less than God one's ultimate concern. However, that which might otherwise be a mortal sin becomes only a venial sin when it is committed in ignorance, or in weakness without the full consent of the will. On the other hand,

> venial sin does disorder but does not constitute a full rupture with God. It is illogical with the sinner who nevertheless remains attached to God but who acts contrary to God. Venial sin may lead to mortal sin. It robs the soul of strength and weakens it for temptation, and it retards progress.[19]

Thus it becomes evident that souls guilty of unremitted mortal sins have no part in purgatory. Their lot is everlasting damnation in hell, in the theology of Catholicism. Those who committed venial sins for which they were forgiven before death enter purgatory for the cleansing of their natures from the effects of sins committed, and from original sin, in preparation for the beautiful vision of God in heaven, through their purgatorial sufferings.

It appears that it is only by the extended grace of God to souls in purgatory that they are able to endure their purifying sufferings. Thus, St. Caesarius is reported to have declared that purgatorial punishments would exceed any sufferings imaginable in the present life.[20] It has been previously noted that their sufferings consist both of a kind of physical or sense suffering inflicted by material fire, and spiritual suffering occasioned not by regret or remorse, but by the soul's intense and insatiable longing for the Holy God. Thus it seems that there is a sort of purging away of the dross or the residue of the evil inhering in physical nature by the fires of purgatory, on the one hand, and a purification of the spiritual nature by the drawing out of the essence of the soul from its evil encasement through its intense longing to see God in pure holiness. The first has a negative effect; the second, a positive. The first would seem to prepare the body, or at least the physical nature of man, for the resurrection of the just. The second prepares the spiritual nature for its confrontation with the Holy God.

Suffering for the deceased in purgatory by Christians still living is an aspect of the Roman Catholic Church's practice that has remained constant. This very obviously means that there is help in sufferings of living saints for the souls in purgatory.

It seems clear that there is no waiting period after death before the Christian enters purgatory. "The non-purified elect pass through purgatory immediately after death, and . . . the damned enter the punishment the moment their souls are no longer able to repent."[21]

Reparation in purgatory springs from penance and from satisfaction made for sin. The "saved sinner" in purgatory is declared to make reparation by entering into the ways of repentance and by returning to God through penance volitionally accepted. This is a sort of liquidation of sin that leads to reparation.[22]

Present Status of the Doctrine of Purgatory

Karl Adam[23] treats the dogma of purgatory with candor and confidence for the modern Catholic mind. However, it is Romano Guardini[24, 25] who, probably better than any other modern Catholic writer, has analyzed the contemporary mind psychologically and reinterpreted the traditional Catholic dogma of purgatory in a way that makes it more palatable to present-day thought.

This contemporary treatment of the dogma of purgatory is characterized by a noticeably lessened emphasis upon the traditional and scriptural foundations, and an increased emphasis upon psychological factors. On the basis of this psychological perspective Guardini[26] regards man as a creature of natural necessity. However, he further views him as a person addressed by God's will and under responsibility to freely fulfill that will. God's will obliges, but does not compel him to obedience. However, after death, the scene changes. No more human freedom exists. In God's holy presence man stands judged, and thus his true being is determined and his destiny is decided. In this sense God judges man, and in this final judgment man is accepted or rejected.

According to Guardini, the good and the evil and the right and the wrong in man are so "intertwined at every point down to the deepest roots"[27] that they cannot be clearly separated in this life. He proceeds to say that while God's judgment after death is final in its fundamental decision, the opportunity to be cleansed from the residue of sin is available to

> the chaotic and fragmentary human existence. Time, as it were, will be extended into eternity long enough for true justice to be satisfied. The man whose good intention God accepts, but whose life as a whole is not free from evil, will, by purging, be brought to a state that fits him for eternal life.[28]

Guardini sees justification completed in purgatorial sanctification. While intention, in the final analysis, determines whether a man is good or evil, yet that intention can reach only as far as man is conscious. Beyond consciousness lies the realm of the unknown. Only the judgment of God's condemning holiness after death can bring to the full light of consciousness the hidden subconscious evil nature, as also the corrupting results of overt sins. Thus this after-death revelation of the real and true nature of man brings to light his *sinful being,* as the Cross has before death at his conversion brought to light his *sinful doings.*[29]

According to Guardini, the divine demand is that the individual progress from goodness inwrought by forgiveness and regeneration at the cross of Christ, to perfection accomplished through purgatorial purification, on to sainthood as the result of this purging. Guardini states that "what is demanded is the final fusion which makes the good man into the perfect man — perfect as 'the Father in Heaven is perfect.' "[30] However, he thinks that "in its full meaning, being good is an endless process."[31] If by this "endless process" he refers to the negative aspect of purification, man would be in a serious, if not hopeless, condition. However, if it is an "endless process" of growth and development of a finally purified personality, then that difficulty disappears.

In defense of purgatorial purification, Guardini argues that while conversion changes man's nature and attitude, it does not eventuate in a purified or sanctified experience in the present life. He states that "though God is almighty He is not a magician. God's laws fashion anew, but fashion in reality. He gives a 'new heart' and a 'new life.' But what has been done has not been undone. Here is a gap that has to be filled. There must be change, purification, preparation."[32]

Guardini frankly admits that the ideas of death and purgatorial purification have largely lost this meaning for the modern, educated, scientifically minded man.

Karl Adam appears more disposed to a scriptural basis for his support of the purgatorial dogma. He asserts, dubiously, that "the Catholic doctrine of Purgatory has no affinity with the Platonic and Origenist view, of Eastern derivation, whereby the human soul embarks after death upon a new stage of its development."[33]

Adam allows that death itself may be the instrument of sanctification and the door to sainthood for a few exceptional souls, but for the most part purgatory is necessary to complete the soul's sanctification.

Evaluation of the Doctrine of Purgatory

There are certain positive criticisms of certain aspects of this doctrine that must, in the interest of fairness, be frankly stated. *First,* the Roman Catholic concept of sin is, for the most part at least, in agreement with both human reason and the Scriptures. This is especially true of overt sin.

Second, the Roman Catholic doctrines of the divine justice and mercy and the atonement of Christ for man's forgiveness are in relatively close agreement with orthodox Protestant views.

Third, the Catholic concept of the holiness of God, and of the necessity of man's holiness to face the holy God, is acceptable to the orthodox Protestant mind.

Fourth, Catholic ideas of the future life of the redeemed in heaven, and of the ultimately damned in hell, seem to meet the traditional orthodox Protestant standards of interpretation.

Fifth, certainly modern Roman Catholic thought has psychoanalyzed well the human personality in the light of the effects of sin upon it.

On the other hand, certain negative criticisms are due the Roman Church in relation to this dogma. *First,* the doctrine of "creationism," as opposed to "traducianism," in relation to the origin of each individual soul, has inescapably relegated the transmission of original sin to the physical. Thus sin is logically posited in matter or the flesh, notwithstanding the Roman Catholic denials of this fact. This made their position an easy prey to the erroneous influences of the Neo-Platonic, the Gnostic, as perhaps also Hindu, concept of sinful matter that contributed largely to asceticism and monasticism, as also celibacy in the priesthood, and the monastery and nunnery. This in turn contributed directly to the notion of the purification of the flesh from sin and its effects through asceticism, good works, sufferings in this life, and the necessity of the purging of the body, as also the soul, from sin in purgatory after death.

A *second* criticism of Roman Catholic thought relative to purgatory falls on their limited concept of the atonement. They do indeed see in Christ's atonement provision for the imperfect forgiveness of sin. However, their concept of the atonement does not provide for the cleansing of the sinful nature of man or his perfection in sanctification. Therefore the works of man, including suffering, are enlisted to complete his salvation. Thus man is saved in part by Christ and in part by humanistic endeavor.

In the *third* place death itself is allowed to be the instrument of sanctification for certain souls well advanced in grace when they meet life's end. This would make death, which is man's enemy, rather than the atonement of Christ, man's final savior.

Fourth, the purgatorial doctrine has contributed heavily to certain superstitions about life after death and the interrelation of the dead with the living. Thus it has fostered a mercenary spirit in the priesthood.

Fifth, it has influenced, practically, careless conduct in the present life by denying the present efficacy of Christ's atonement for the totality of human sin, and by extending hope for sin's ultimate remedy into the life to come.

Sixth, the purgatorial doctrine has left the Christian in a present state of hopeless sinful entanglement to engross his interest and efforts, who should be free in Christ for devotion to active service for God in this life.

Seventh, the doctrine rests on no clear or sure scriptural foundation, and thus has no adequate basis.

End Notes

CHAPTER III

[1]*A Catholic Dictionary* (The Catholic Encyclopedic Dictionary) Donald Attwater, ed., 2nd ed., rev. (New York: Macmillan, 1949), pp. 413, 414.

[2]*Theological Library, The Historical and Mystical Christ,* A.M. Henry, ed., trans. by Angeline Bouchard (Chicago: Fidec Publishers Association, 1958), V:468.

[3]Henry Dominic Denzinger, *The Sources of Catholic Dogma (St. Louis: B. Herder Book Co., 1957), pp. 242, 243, pars. 778-780.*

[4]*A Catholic Dictionary,* p. 413.

[5]Winfred Ernest Garrison, *A Protestant Manifesto* (New York: Abingdon-Cokesbury Press, 1952), pp. 158, 159.

[6]Ibid., p. 159.   [7]Ibid.   [8]Ibid.

[9]*Theological Library,* V:468.   [10]Ibid.

[11]Denzinger, *Sources of Catholic Dogma,* pp. 219, 220, par. 693.

[12]*Theological Library,* V:468.

[13]Denzinger, *Sources of Catholic Dogma,* p. 261, par. 840.

[14]Ibid., p. 298, par. 983.

[15]Karl Adam, *One and Only.* (Used with permission of Sheed and Ward, 115 E. Armour Blvd., Kansas City, MO, 1957), p. 22.

[16]Ibid., pp. 22, 23.   [17]*Theological Library,* V:262.

[18]Ibid.   [19]Ibid.   [20]Ibid., V:468.

[21]Ibid., V:471.   [22]Ibid., III:260.

[23]Karl Adam, *The Spirit of Catholicism* (New York: Macmillan, 1952).

[24]Romano Guardini, *The Faith and Modern Man* (New York: Pantheon Books, 1952).

[25]Romano Guardini, *The Last Things.* Translators, Charlotte E. Forsythe & Grace B. Branhan (New York: Pantheon Books, A Division of Random House, Inc. © 1954. Used by permission).

[26]Ibid., p. 33.   [27]Ibid., p. 35.   [28]Ibid.   [29]Ibid., p. 42.

[30]Ibid.   [31]Ibid.   [32]Ibid., pp. 44, 45.

[33]Adam, *Spirit of Catholicism,* p. 115.

Chapter IV
The Life Everlasting, or Christian Immortality

"And this is eternal life [zoe], *that they may know Thee the only true God, and Jesus Christ whom Thou hast sent"* (John 17:3).

Introduction

Millenniums ago Job voiced the curiosity of the human mind concerning the future life in his immortal words: "If a man dies, will he live again?" (Job 14:14). Throughout the history of the human race men of all nationalities, religions and philosophies have sought, in one way or another, to find the answer to that question. There are but two exceptions to this attitude of mind toward man's future hope. The one is represented by the ancient Jewish sect of the Sadducees and the other by certain sophisticates of every enlightened age. The first is organizationally dead and the second is intellectually and spiritually dead. The significant lines of Pascal bear testimony to this fact. "The immortality of the soul is a thing so important that only those who have lost all feeling can rest indifferent to it, can be content to know if it is not, or if it is."[1]

On the survival of the soul after physical death, S. E. Frost writes:

> . . . the human mind has never been content to let the matter rest here. Throughout the history

of mankind there has persisted a conviction, sometimes divine and at other times very vivid, that death cannot be the end, that the grave is not a victory of man's foes, that death does not inflict a cosmic sting. In every age there have been millions firm in the belief that what is truest in humanity persists in some form or state after death.[2]

The idea of immortality is one of those fundamental concepts of the human mind that forbids it to rest until it rests in a valid answer to this age-old question raised by Job.

Dietrich Bonhoeffer[3] argues that atheistic unbelief is the ultimate of sin which so completely excludes God from man's life that it embraces in itself all other sins, and thus even suicide or any other act adds nothing to the guilt of such a man outside of God's claims upon his life (see John 16:7-9; Rom. 14:23).

The words of Christ are highly significant at the outset of any consideration of Christian immortality. Said He: "And this is eternal life, that they may know Thee the only true God, and Jesus Christ whom Thou has sent" (John 17:3); and again: "I came that they might have life, and might have it abundantly" (John 10:10b); and yet again: "I give eternal life to them" (John 10:28a; see also John 3:16, 36; 6:54; Rom. 6:23; John 1:1-14; 1 Thess. 5:23).

The sincerely concerned, wealthy young Jewish ruler who came running to Christ voiced his quest in the words, "What shall I do to inherit eternal life?" (Mark 10:17b). The conceited Jewish lawyer, with the purpose to ensnare Jesus in His own words, voiced the question, "Teacher, what shall I do to inherit eternal life?" (Luke 10:25b).

Christian Immortality: What Is It?

Dagobert E. Runes states that the word "immortality" is derived from the Latin negative prefix *in* (not) plus the Latin root *mortalis* (mortal). Taken together the result is "not mortal," or not subject to death. Runes then proceeds to give the following formal definition of immortality:

> The doctrine that the soul or personality of man survives the death of the body. The two principal conceptions of immortality are: (a) *temporal immortality,* the indefinite continuation of the individual mind after death and (b) *eternity,* ascension of the soul to a higher plane of timelessness.[4]

It is our present purpose to treat the idea of immortality *per se* in its Christian meaning. Thus, immortality will be regarded here as that doctrine that the soul or personality of believing man begins at conversion and survives the death of the body, and transforms the soul to a higher plane of timelessness. Again, the idea of immortality here will be restricted to the present and post-existence, or life after death, as opposed to pre-existence, which is not a Christian doctrine. Thus, the person will be regarded as everlastingly conscious and identical, but not eternal, in the sense of being uncreated.

The Origin of Human Personality

The problem of the origin of human souls or self-conscious personalities is very old and somewhat complex. The traditional Roman Catholic position, and a position held by some Protestant thinkers even today, maintains that all souls are directly created by God at conception. God, according to this position, cooperates in the human act of procreation by furnishing a divinely created soul for the humanly procreated body. Thus, in this view, the soul as an entity is divinely created and added to the body at conception. Paul J. Glenn[5], a Roman Catholic scholar, makes clear this position. He holds that God directly creates the soul of each child at conception and adds it to the body of the fetus, which body is physically procreated through conception by the parents.

Glenn's position, called *creationism,* is fraught with many insurmountable difficulties. Of the many, only two of the most important need concern us here.

The first problem, the inheritance of "original sin," or "depravity," is not the least of the difficulties involved in the theory of *creationism.* St. Augustine, in his later years, saw the difficulty and concluded that in some manner the soul of the child must proceed from the souls of the parents. Augustine's position is known as *traducianism.* Glenn objects seriously to Augustine's position and attempts to evade the dilemma by substituting a third factor, which he designates "human nature," a kind of scapegoat for inherited depravity.

The second serious problem in the theory of *creationism* is that of involving God in objectionable unethical cooperation. Ethically forbidden cohabitation in extramarital relations is frequently biologically productive. If God is the creator of each soul directly at conception then it becomes quite clear that He could not retain His moral integrity while cooperating with His creatures in the commission of an immoral act. Since God's moral integrity would be thus violated, the ethical idea of God would necessarily be degraded and the holiness of God would be thereby cancelled. The far-reaching implications of this ethically and theologically embarrassing consideration are not difficult to imagine.

What then is the origin of the soul? There seems to be but one satisfactory answer to the question. That answer is found in the book of Genesis. There it is stated that "God created man in His own image, in the image of God He created him; male and female He created them" (Gen. 1:27). Then further, the writer of Genesis explains, "The Lord God formed man of dust from the ground, and breathed into his nostrils the breath of life; and man became a living being" (Gen. 2:7). Following this account of creation, the author of Genesis appears to make clear God's plan and purpose in the human procreative process.

> And God blessed them; and God said to them, "Be fruitful and multiply, and fill the earth, and subdue it; and rule over the fish of the sea and over the birds of the sky, and over every living thing that moves on the earth" (Gen. 1:28; cf. Ps. 8:3-8).

Obviously, when God created man (generically) He endowed him with the higher spiritual principle of ever-lasting conscious personality, and then committed to him the tremendous responsibility, but also the challenging and glorious privilege, of procreating himself, body and soul, or personality, as a unitary being, functionally, though his body is chemically compounded. Man was quite evidently a divinely effected synthesis of *dust* and the *breath* of God. God "breathed into his nostrils the breath of life; and man became a *living being*" (Gen. 2:7). It is not to be overlooked that this conclusion implies the necessity of the "bodily form" for the identity and expression of the person. Paul's argument is clear and convincing in favor of the necessity of a bodily resurrection for *personal identity,* as also for divine victory over physical death (*see* 1 Cor. 15:37-44).

Hence it is both scripturally and humanly logical to conclude that at conception there emerges a new entity from the synthesis of the parents, and that each new emergent is an everlasting self-conscious spiritual personality. Accordingly, man is endowed with the power of procreating the soul or personality, as well as the body of the child, and thus the otherwise unsolvable problems inhering in the theory of *creationism* are eliminated and man is dignified by God-given self-re-creative powers. His responsibility for the right use of those powers also becomes very great.

In the light of these considerations, the only logically consistent position seems to be that of *traducianism,* as advocated by St. Augustine, notwithstanding the fact that Augustine was unable to make clear the "how" of this unitary procreation of man. Thus the first spiritual unitary (or holistic) personality had its origin in the creative act of God. But all subsequent personalities have had their origins in man's divinely delegated procreative powers, as unitary, holistic persons, functionally.

Christian Immortality Distinguished From Other Concepts of Futurity

First, the concept of Christian immortality for believing mankind, as previously defined, must be clearly differentiated from the idea of *eternal.* Christian *immortality,* though begun at conversion, looks to a blissful, endless future existence of conscious personalities in relation to and contingent upon God. Eternal conveys the idea of timelessness, both in the past and in the future. Eternal, as applied to immortal conscious personalities, would imply that such personalities were uncreated. If they were uncreated, they would not be contingent upon God. If they were not contingent upon God, they would be self-existent, and if they were self-existent, they would be divine, and divinity does not belong to humanity.

Second, the Christian concept of immortality must be clearly differentiated from the Oriental view of *pre-existence, transmigration of souls,* and the doctrine of *Karma,* all three of which doctrines are inseparably linked together. Pre-existence of souls has taken different forms in various schools of thought. The best known and most representative doctrines of pre-existence are those of Plato, Plotinus, and the Hindus of India. To these views it may be of interest to add the Mormon view, which differs from the foregoing only in certain respects.

A third idea that must be clearly distinguished from the Christian concept of immortality, as the idea is considered here, is that of a *temporary life after death.* This view would be, in the very nature of the case, limited immortality rather than Christian immortality. It is a view that was held, concerning the souls of both the gods and men, by certain of the Greek and Roman thinkers, and it is a view held by many primitive and other pagan peoples in the world today, including the Ona Indians of South America.

Again, the Christian doctrine of immortality must be clearly differentiated from *conditional immortality,* as taught by the religious philosopher William Ernest Hocking of Harvard University, a sort of "take it or leave it at will" doctrine, or William James's "Will to Believe." It must also be disassociated from the doctrine of *annihilationism,* usually applied to the complete extinction of the wicked at death, or as held by some, at the final judgment. But by others, especially certain materialists such as Bertrand Russell, it has been applied to *all* future existence. The Russellites and the Seventh Day Adventists have been strong advocates of the former view, i.e., for the wicked.

Finally, while it is not the purpose here to treat extensively the Old Testament views of immortality, those views do indeed lie back of the Christian doctrine as found in the New Testament. The early Hebrews and later Pharasaic Jews appear to have progressively grasped the doctrine of immortality – often very faintly understood, but at other times with remarkable insight they anticipated the Christian doctrine. Except for a few notable insights, such as Job, Isaiah, and Daniel, this doctrine appears to have reached its clearest understanding by the Jews during the Inter-Testament period, just prior to the Christian era.

The Christian Doctrine of Immortality *Per Se*

The orthodox Christian doctrine of immortality stands alone and unique among the many other ideas of the soul's destiny in its teaching concerning the future of the redeemed. There appear to be three significant advances in Christian thought over the Jewish concept of a future life: (1) the emphasis upon individual immortality becomes clearer, though individual relation to the group or nation is also important; (2) the idea of the resurrection becomes clearly evident; and (3) the nature of the future life becomes more distinct and explicit.

First, Jesus taught the *kingdom of heaven* as a community of the redeemed on earth, but so constituted as to be capable of everlasting continuance. Although the individual is a member of the spiritual kingdom, he stands also in direct personal relation with God. Indeed, Christ perfected the idea of the individual and brought it forth into a clearer light than at any previous time. Here there emerges the provision of both an immortal spiritual individual and an immortal spiritual community of the redeemed.

Second, while Job, Ezekiel, Daniel and Isaiah all caught faint glimpses of immortality through a bodily resurrection, it remained for Christ and Paul to explain this great doctrine more clearly.

Logically, a future life of everlasting bliss could be realized only through the reconciliation of man with God. Since God only, and not the human personality, is infinite, it follows that for immortality, as herein defined, the finite human person is contingent upon the infinite personality of God. The experience of sin had made such a relationship impossible of attainment for man, apart from divine intervention. A Mediator was required for the reconciliation of guilty and alienated man with the pure and holy being of God. Such a Mediator must be, in the very nature of the case, both divine and human. Hence the necessity of the incarnation of God in man, the God-Man, Christ Jesus. The incarnation and atoning death of Jesus Christ would have been incomplete for redemptive purposes without the resurrection and ascension. The assumption of human nature by divinity, the substitutionary death of Christ, and His bodily resurrection and ascension, bridged the great gulf between man's alienated soul and God; and thus Christ afforded a way for alienated man to return to an everlasting blissful relationship with God. Christ said, "I am the way, and the truth, and the life; no one comes to the Father, but through Me" (John 14:6). Again Christ said, "I am the resurrection and the life; he who believes in Me shall live even if he dies, and everyone who lives and believes in Me shall never die" (John 11:25-26).

Paul makes this doctrine of the "resurrection unto life" explicit in 1 Corinthians 15. It was also the very heart of the message of the apostolic Christians, as that message is recorded in the Acts of the Apostles. In Christ was furnished the means for the realization of the individual and personal immortality toward which the mind of man had ever persistently striven, but to which it had never been able to attain unaided by divine revelation. The ascended Christ's words as recorded in the Revelation are significant at this juncture: "I am the first and the last, and the living One; and I was dead, and behold, I am alive forevermore, and I have the keys of death and of Hades" (Rev. 1:17-18). Christ's authority over death and the grave is the assurance of believing man's immortality.

Third, there remains much unrevealed concerning the nature of immortality in the Christian teaching. Nevertheless it becomes evident that immortal life in the future is unending, and that it is entirely free from the experience of sin with its woeful consequences. Also it is characterized by personal identity and consciousness, and a *spiritual bodily form* is provided for the personal identity of the immortal spirit. And it is evident that endless growth in God's grace and infinite progress will continue. This is made clear in Paul's first letter to the Corinthians, chapter 15. It is further evident, from the teachings of the apostles, especially, that the finite redeemed and immortal soul will experience a continual progressive development toward the infinite character of God throughout the aeons (see Heb. 12:22-24). On this question Wesley says: "Yet he still grows in grace and in the knowledge of Christ, and in the love and image of God, and will do so, not only till death but probably to all eternity."[6]

Although the idea of immortality may not be empirically demonstrable, it may be and has been courageously believed by millions of people since the days of Christ.

The Necessary Grounds for Christian Immortality

The necessary grounds for a satisfactory concept of immortality may be considered in a sixfold manner.

First, the everlasting moral freedom of human personality is requisite to personal immortality. Since only spiritual persons are morally free, and since moral freedom is requisite to spiritual personality, then it follows that if spiritual personality is to experience immortality it must retain a degree of moral freedom. To deprive a person of moral freedom would mean the cancellation of an essential note of human personality which would, in turn, reduce one to a robot, and Christ redeems persons, not robots.

Second, rational consciousness must ever characterize the immortal person. Since rationality is an essential characteristic of spiritual persons, differentiating them from all lower forms of life, it follows that if personal immortality is to be experienced, rationality must ever characterize the person. This is that "something" a person has that is closely akin to God. Says Paul concerning the new man of redemption: he "is being *renewed to a true knowledge* according to the image of the One who created him" (Col. 3:10).

A *third* necessary ground for immortality is moral responsibility. Moral responsibility is the direct consequent of personal freedom and rationality. Therefore, while personality remains rational and free it will be morally responsible.

Freedom without responsibility is always dangerous and will eventually be self-destructive, as also destructive of the best interest of others. Responsibility places the necessary limitations on human freedom.

A *fourth* necessary ground for personal immortality is the indestructibility of the soul. Plato argued the indestructibility of the soul on the ground of its simplicity as opposed to the compound. If it has no parts, said Plato, then it cannot be dissolved. Although Plato's argument has been challenged, it will be evident that if the soul is to be immortal it must be indestructible. Perhaps the greater weight of evidence for the indestructibility of the soul rests in the fact that spiritual personalities are ends in themselves, rather than means to ends. Therefore, as ultimates in God's plan, they are in the very nature of the case indestructible. Could personalities – individuals – possibly be the true atoms of the universe?

A *fifth* ground of personal immortality is improvability. Personality is spiritual. Spirit is always active. Activity for the redeemed bespeaks purposeful progress, for a rational, free, moral person could not remain active without purposeful progression. Cessation of activity would result in spiritual annihilation, and annihilation is not a tenable doctrine. Morality requires purposeful or worthy ends, and therefore the activity must be directed toward a worthy end. That end is the further development of immortal personality in Christ. Paul seems to have grasped this idea at the close of his master-work on love. Said he, "But now abide faith, hope, love, these three; but the greatest of these is love" (1 Cor. 13:13). Someone has observed that by faith comes anticipation; by hope, apprehension; and by love, appreciation, or enjoyment. Thus considered, these are the three virtues necessary to the unending progressive enrichment of the immortal person in Christ.

A *sixth* necessary ground for immortality is the existence of a moral sphere. If a moral sphere is presently necessary for the self-realization and continuance of moral personality, then in order for the continuance of moral responsibility, in the endless future, the universe must of necessity afford an infinite moral arena. Such a moral universe inhabited by free rational moral persons, in relation to and dependent upon God, cannot be logically a realm of closed moral probation. The absence of evil and temptation does not imply the absence of man's moral freedom. If such were the case then there could have been no original sin, in the sense of a *first* unethical act. L. S. Keyser has said: "Sin is an eternal possibility, but never an eternal necessity."[7]

Should it be objected that such a position would allow for a "second-chance Fall" of redeemed man after death, it should be noted that the following factors would preclude such an eventuality. (1) All actual sin and temptation, in the sense of enticement by a tempter, will be absent; (2) redeemed man will live in the light of the total effects of the Fall and of God's redeeming love that provided his deliverance from sin and its consequences through reconciliation to God in Christ; (3) his love and devotion to God will be not only a personal, historical decision, but a *continuous* choice of love, devotion, and service to God.

The foregoing may be considered somewhat analogous to the successful continuous marriage relation. At a point in history a man and woman make their mutual choice of each other, seal that choice by matrimony, and then throughout life continue to choose one another momentarily. Divorce is always possible, and much as it is deplored, few would wish it to be legally impossible. Certainly the marriage relation is more meaningful by reason of the continuous mutual choices of the partners throughout life, growing in mutual appreciation and enrichment with the fuller and deeper knowledge and understanding of each other, than were they compelled legally or otherwise to remain together.

Likewise, it would seem reasonable that redeemed man's continuous loving choice of God, both here and hereafter, would be more meaningful to both God and man than if man were deprived of his moral freedom and thus reduced to a redeemed robot. Nor does there appear to be any valid support in the Scriptures for the age-old teaching that redeemed man will be deprived of moral choice in the hereafter. Indeed, emphasis upon death as the closed door of probation has been highly effective in decision-getting in evangelistic preaching. Such emphasis, however, does not of necessity make the teaching reasonable or scripturally valid.

The part played by death in relation to the "fixedness of man's destiny" may be illustrated, as one has said (and in full consideration of the limitations of the comparison), by the photographer's chemical bath that sets the image in the print. It is the decision of man's rational will that sets the image, or determines his destiny, either for heaven or hell, rather than the arbitrary will of God. Adam Clarke has well said that a Christian goes to heaven because Christ died for him; a sinner goes to hell because he deserves to go there.

In either case, his destiny is the result of his moral, or immoral, choice, in the acceptance or rejection of Christ's provision of salvation, and not the arbitrary will of God. In either destiny, man's moral choice will be so self-determined as to preclude any possibility that he will ever change his mind or course of direction after death. Both the redeemed and the unredeemed are so constituted personally as to be indestructible individuals in the sense of annihilation. The redeemed will experience continued progressive enrichment and development of their finite personalities in relation to the infinite personality of God, both here and hereafter. The unredeemed will, on the contrary, progressively degenerate into lower and lower stages of depravity without the possibility of ever experiencing annihilation in the world to come.

The Validity of Christian Immortality

Certain fundamental reasons for the necessity of immortality to satisfy the human mind are noteworthy.

First, nothing short of immortality, with its implications for the present and future life, will satisfy the demands of a person's moral nature for a sense of justice not realized in the present life.

Second, immortality is required for the fuller realization of the development of personality not possible of attainment in the present life. The awakening of a person's mind to the vastness and richness of an infinite universe within the brief span of a lifetime cannot logically terminate with a sudden cessation of personal existence. Such a consideration would be disillusioning and destructive of the value and worthfulness of the present life.

In the *third* instance, it is evident that immortality is necessary to the very nature of redeemed personality. The personalities of God and human persons created in His image are the only ultimate realities in the universe. They are the only entities that exist of and for their own ends. All else is contingent upon personalities and exists for those persons. In other words, all else besides persons possesses only *instrumental value.* Persons have *intrinsic* value. Finally, to destroy all persons, including God, would mean cessation of all existence. The fallacy of such a conclusion is self-evident.

Fourth, the reason that immortality is essential to the nature of personality grows out of a consideration of the creativity of human personality. What man creates in the realm of social and moral values through constructive thinking and activity enriches life, and in a sense the universe itself. As the universe created by God is contingent for its existence upon the Creator, so are the values created by men contingent upon their creators. Thus, the cessation of existence would be destructive of all values inhering in the creative personalities. Such a disposal of values would not be worthy of the character of God.

A *fifth* reason the nature of personality does not admit of annihilation is that it is spiritual, and as such it is ever active. While it remains spiritual, it cannot become inert and thus cease to exist. Hence, the nature of personality as ultimate, creative, and active, logically establishes the necessity of its immortality.

Sixth, the immortality of human personality rests on the necessity of the fulfillment of the purpose of creation. To say that man was created good is to say that God had a good end in view for him. Otherwise, there would be the dilemma of a morally good, spiritual personality existing for no good purpose in the universe. Furthermore, such a purpose as would be worthy of the free moral personality of man could not be logically realized within time. Only the contemplation of timelessness could possibly satisfy such an intellectual and spiritual demand.

Seventh, the validity of immortality is attested by the demand for the fulfillment of the purpose of redemption. When the cost and the intricacy of the divine plan of redemption are contemplated, the mind revolts at the thought of an ultimate cessation of the existence of spiritual personalities redeemed at such great cost and care.

Eighth, and finally, the immortality of man is necessary to the satisfaction of the divine desire for personal fellowship. Love is the very essence of God. But love demands an object upon which to bestow itself, an object which must be capable of response to its overtures. Impersonal creation is incapable of thus responding. Therefore, God requires personal beings for the full satisfaction of His own nature. Paul speaks of "the riches of the glory of *His* [God's] *inheritance* in the saints" (Eph. 1:18). Anything short of such a conception of God would resolve itself into something comparable to Aristotle's idea of God as the "unmoved mover." A personal, loving God could have no pleasure in a lonely self-existence. Nor could He have pleasure in the temporary enjoyment of the fellowship of His redeemed creatures only to snuff out their existence eventually. If God is personal, His nature demands the everlasting personal fellowship of human personalities whom He has created and lovingly redeemed, and who have freely chosen Him for their everlasting companionship.

The Source of Christian Immortality

Eternal life, or immortality, was resident in man before the Fall through God's indwelling Spirit, but it was lost through the greatest of all world tragedies – the Fall. The Genesis account informs us that "the Lord God . . . breathed into his nostrils the breath of life; and man became a living being" (Gen. 2:7). When man disobeyed God and separated himself from Him, he lost this divinely endowed immortality. God then set a boundary upon him by removing him from the Garden where he had access to the Tree of Life, lest he should eat of that tree and live forever in his sin and alienation from God (Gen. 3:22).

Jesus Christ, as God incarnate, is now the only source of eternal life open to man. Paul declared that Divinity "alone *possesses immortality* and dwells in unapproachable light." J. B. Phillips translates this passage thus: "God . . . the only *source of immortality*" (1 Tim. 6:16; cf. Rom. 6:23). Jesus Christ is man's only access to divine immortality, or eternal life. Paul states that "the free gift of God is eternal life in Christ Jesus our Lord" (Rom. 6:23b).

Wesley states that:

> . . . God hath given us, not only a title to, but the real beginning of, eternal life: And this life is purchased by, and treasured up in, his Son; who hath all the springs and fullness of it in himself, to communicate to his body, the Church. This eternal life then commences when it pleases the Father to reveal his Son in our hearts; when we first know

Christ, being enabled to "call him Lord by the Holy Ghost." . . . Then it is that heaven is opened in the soul, that the proper heavenly state commences . . . our knowledge and our love of him increases, by the same degrees, and in the same proportion, the kingdom of an inward heaven must necessarily increase also; while we "grow up in all things into Him who is our Head."[8]

On the necessity of the impartation of the divine life, as opposed to mere imputation, for the realization of the everlasting life or immortality of the believer, Wesley is very specific and emphatic. He declares,

None shall live with God, but he that now lives to God; none shall enjoy the glory of God in heaven, but he that bears the image of God on earth; none that is not saved from sin here can be saved from hell hereafter; none can see the kingdom of God above, unless the kingdom of God be in him below. Whosoever will reign with Christ in heaven, must have Christ reigning in him on earth . . .[9]

The Meaning of Christian Immortality

Eternal life is primarily qualitative, though it is also consequently quantitative. Geddes MacGregor[10] observes that there are three words used in the Greek New Testament to express the various kinds of life. The first is *biós,* which refers to the life span, the temporary vitalizing principle of a natural organism, and from which we get our word *biology.* The second word is *psyche,* which indicates the animating principle, and from which we get our English word *psychology.* Third, there is the word *zoë,* which signifies a higher quality of life, and is the principal word used for immortality in the New Testament, especially in John's writings. In the New Testament this *zoë,* or *eternal life,* is declared to be the result of one's having been born again (John 3:3). It is the consequent of putting on Christ in Galatians 3:27; it is the result of being quickened together with Christ in Ephesians 2:5; it is the consequent of being in Christ in 2 Corinthians 5:17; it results from *putting on the new man* in Ephesians 4:24; and of being a new creature in Christ in Galatians 6:15. It is significant that *zoë* is generally used with the definite article in the Greek New Testament, and thus indicates that the readers must have been quite familiar with the concept of what it signified.

This *zoë,* or *eternal life,* in the New Testament is the supreme blessing of God mediated to men by Jesus Christ. It is the *very quality* of God's life given to believing man by Jesus Christ. The Old Testament is, for the most part, concerned primarily with life as "length of days on earth" — such as "three score years and ten." The New Testament and Christianity are concerned primarily with the quality of the life that lasts, rather than the span of years during which one may exist through animation by the life provided by God and nature. Christ said that He came that men might have life, and "might have it abundantly" (John 10:10). The life of Christ is an infinite, divine energy which transcends all forms of empirical or sensible manifestations. It is God's life in Christ imparted by the Spirit to the true believer. "I give eternal life to them," said Jesus, "and they shall *never* perish" (John 10:28).

Quantitative life *per se* could never be adequate for man's fullest self-realization. George Paget Thompson, Nobel prize-winning scientist, suggests that natural life may be extended, or old age may eventually be postponed indefinitely through improved medical science. Should this scientific achievement be realized the following conditions, among others, would result. First, all death would be either accidental or voluntary. Second, life insurance would have to be converted to immortality insurance. Third, sickness or disability might be prolonged indefinitely. Fourth, if man lived 500 years there would be no reason to believe that he would be any nearer to the realization of his life's goals at 499 years than he is now at 79 or 80 years of age. Fifth, on the other hand, the longer span might give some persons more time to make a greater shipwreck of life, and incidentally, it would considerably increase the tax burden to provide Social Security for man from the present retirement age of 62 or 65 years to the 500-year mark.

MacGregor[11] observes that there are many noted witnesses to the value and superiority of qualitative over quantitative life. Benjamin Franklin said in *Poor Richard,* "Wish not so much to live long as to live well." Ralph Waldo Emerson said, "It is the depth at which we live and not at all the surface extension that imports" (*Society and Solitude,* "Works and Days"). Crabbe stated: "Life is not to be measured by the time we live" (*The Village,* Book II). Sallust, the Roman historian, said, "No parent would wish for his children that they might live forever, but rather that their lives might be good and honorable" (*Jurgurtha,* Chap. 85, Sec. 50). Seneca said, "The wise man will live as long as he ought, and not as long as he can, for he is always thinking about the quality, not the quantity of his life" (*Epist. ad Lucilium,* 70, 4).

The Effects of Christian Immortality

Eternal life has exceedingly large and significant effects on the present life of man. First, it awakens the natural life (*biós*) and the innate potential of persons and causes them to germinate and grow, just as the warmth of the sun stimulates germination in the seed and causes it to spring into new life and fruition. Second, it unites the eternal life of God in Christ (*Zoë*) with the natural life of man (*biós*) in the conversion experience, and thus lifts man to a higher level of life and living here and now, but which will continue forever.

As an illustration of the foregoing principle, one might consider a box of seed placed in the dark basement where there are objects painted with luminous paint in each of the four corners of the room. With the box in the center of the room, as the seed sprouted and grew, the plants would bend in four different directions, depending on their proximity to the luminous objects which would pick up and reflect such light as existed in the otherwise apparent darkness. Should the window blind be slit to let in a beaming ray of sunlight, the plants would all then turn toward the sunlight. Just so, there are many natural objects in the world that reflect the sunlight of God's natural revelation (see Ps. 19), and that appeal to man's natural aspirations and drives.

However, when Christ shines forth on men, He is the true light of God that brings to them spiritual illumination and life everlasting (John 1:9), unless they turn willfully away from Him into outer darkness. If they do so, they will die in their natural sinful state, devoid of this essential quality of eternal life, the life of God in Christ, though they will continue to exist in endless progressive degeneracy.

Eternal life has the effect for the future of an unbroken continuity of the presently experienced divine life. Jesus said, on the occasion of the raising of Lazarus, "Everyone who lives and believes in Me shall never die" (John 11:26b).

Finally, there will be the continued development of the redeemed personality as it moves forever toward the infinite divine perfection, even in the future life (cf. Matt. 5:48). The author of the letter to the Hebrews says concerning the redeemed in the life to come: "You have come . . . to the spirits of righteous men made perfect" (Heb. 12:22a-23b).[12]

End Notes

CHAPTER IV

[1]Quoted by Frederick D. Kershner in *Horizons of Immortality* (St. Louis, MO: Bethany Press, 1926), p. 12.

[2]S. E. Frost, *The Basic Teachings of the Great Philosophers* (Philadelphia: The Blakiston Company, 1942), p. 171.

[3]Dietrich Bonhoeffer, *Ethics,* Eberhard Bethge, ed. (New York: Macmillan, 1965), pp. 166-172.

[4]Dagobert D. Runes, *The Dictionary of Philosophy* (New York: Philosophical Library, 1942), p. 142.

[5]Paul J. Glenn, *An Introduction to Philosophy* (St. Louis, MO: B. Herder Book Company, 1944), pp. 314, 315.

[6]John Wesley, *A Plain Account of Christian Perfection* (Louisville, KY: Pentecostal Publishing Co., n.d.), pp. 24, 25.

[7]L. S. Keyser, *A System of General Ethics* (Burlington, IA: The Lutheran Literary Board, 1934), p. 138.

[8]John Wesley, *The Works of John Wesley* (Grand Rapids: Baker Book House, rep. 1978), 6:430.

[9]Robert W. Burtner and Robert E. Chiles, *A Compend of Wesley's Theology* (Nashville: Abingdon Press, 1957), p. 278.

[10]Geddes MacGregor, *Introduction to Religious Philosophy* (Boston: Houghton Mifflin, 1959), p. 192.

[11]Ibid., p. 192ff.

[12]Much of the material in this chapter appears in the book *From Revival to Evangelism* written by Charles W. Carter (Salem, OH: Schmul Publishing Co., 1986). Used by permission of Harold E. Schmul, president.

Chapter V
Heaven and the Hereafter

What Is The Meaning of Heaven?

Perhaps no item of the Christian faith has been characterized by as much sentimentality as the idea of heaven. Indeed the New Testament, and especially the figurative language of Revelation when taken from its contextual setting, furnishes the basis of much of this unwarranted sentimentality about heaven. Christian songs, poetry, and sermons have all made their contributions to these often unbiblical notions about heaven.

In reality the Bible has much less to say about heaven *per se* than about everlasting life. In fact the biblical words for heaven are often ambiguous if removed from their specific contexts. J. Kenneth Grider states:

> The most frequently used Hebrew word for Heaven in the Old Testament is *šāmayim,* signifying "heaved up things" or "the heights." In the Greek New Testament it is *ouranos,* which denotes "sky," or "air." These words refer to the atmosphere just above the earth (Gen. 1:20, etc.); to the firmament in which the sun, the moon, and the stars are located (Gen. 1:14, etc.); to God

above (Ps. 2:4, etc.); to the abode of the angels (Matt. 22:30). The Old Testament has no word for universe and to express the idea there is the frequent "heaven and earth." We read of "the heaven and the heaven of heavens" (Deut. 10:14), and of a man's being "caught up into the third heaven" (2 Cor. 12:2), but such references are probably to be thought of metaphorically.[1]

Although figurative language in the Bible, as elsewhere, is not to be depreciated, such figures must be understood in context and with a view to the meanings they are intended to convey. In a certain sense all language is figurative. Perhaps the best definition of a word is "the symbol of an idea," and thus a means of communication when the symbol is understood by both the communicator and the recipient.

The Bible is the richest book of all literature in its use of figurative language. S. S. Curry lists among the varied types of biblical literature the following: the narrative . . . the didactic, the oratoric, the allegoric, the lyric, the dramatic, and the epic.[2] Certainly many other types can be added to this list such as the parable, the tragedy, the metaphor, and the Hebrew parallelism.

Although the Old Testament is for the most part vague concerning the nature of the future life, the New Testament leaves us in no doubt concerning the state of the redeemed beyond the present temporal life. Jesus assured His disciples before He left them,

> Let not your heart be troubled; [you, mar.] believe in God, believe also in Me. In My Father's house are many dwelling places; if it were not so, I would have told you; for I go to prepare a place for you. And if I go and prepare a place for you, I will come again, and receive you to Myself; that where I am, there you may be also (John 14:1-3).

Lest there should be any doubt concerning where Christ was going, and where His followers would be with Him in their future lives, the author of the Epistle to the Hebrews assures us that "we have such a high priest [Christ], who has taken His seat at the right hand of the throne of the Majesty [God] in the heavens" (Heb. 8:1). William Barclay translates Peter's words thus:

> It is necessary that heaven should receive Him until the times when all things shall be restored, times of which God spoke through the mouths of His holy prophets since the world began (Acts 3:21).[3]

Paul adds his witness to that of Christ when he says,

> For we know that if the earthly tent which is our house [our physical bodies] is torn down, we have a building from God, a house [a body] not made with hands, eternal in the heavens. . . . For indeed while we are in this tent, we groan, being burdened, because we do not want to be unclothed, but to be clothed, in order that what is mortal may be swallowed up by life (2 Cor. 5:1, 4).

It becomes evident from the foregoing, as also from many other scriptures, that while there is a change from the temporal to the future existence there is also continuity — in fact a personal identity of the present with the future.

Grider states:

> The whole person survives, in the biblical teaching. Even the body is raised again, so that, if it is no longer flesh and blood (1 Cor. 15:50), it nevertheless has a continuity with the present body, a sameness in form if not in material element (see Matt. 5:29-30; 10:28; Rom. 8:11, 23; 1 Cor. 15:53). So there is nothing in the Bible (nor in the main creeds of the church) about disembodied spirits in the next world existing *in vacuo*.[4]

Of one thing we can be certain from God's revelation — the redeemed in heaven will be in the immediate presence of the holy and righteous sovereign God. There the finite redeemed of this life will forever have access to and grow in the personal riches of God's infinite grace and love, and the exhaustless resources of His redeemed universe which He created for humanity's benefit before the tragedy of the Fall. With Paul we are compelled to say, "Now we see in a mirror dimly, but then face to face; now . . . [we] know in part, but then . . . [we] shall know fully just as . . . [we] also have been fully known" (1 Cor. 13:12).

Grider says further:

> They will not so much glory in the presence of the Supreme Reason, as the Greeks anticipated, but in the wonder of the All-Holy One (Isa. 6:3; Rev. 4:8). And this God is a Father, in whose house (John 14:2) the redeemed will dwell, where they shall be His people, and where "God Himself shall be with them" (Rev. 21:3).[5]

Where Is Heaven?

For many, perhaps the location of heaven is one of the most difficult questions of the Christian faith. This problem stems in part, if not in large measure, from the disposition to divide God's universe into the sacred and the secular.

Two extreme and erroneous positions have been held by both many laymen and theologians. On the one hand, for many centuries the universe was divided into *the present evil world below* and *God's holy heaven above.* In this view God had abdicated the temporal evil world, leaving it to the control of Satan and his wicked followers. Accordingly, Christians were redeemed in this evil world and life. They lived as redeemed believers in a world wholly dominated by Satan as the god of this evil order while they labored and longed for *heaven and their eternal home above.*

While there is a certain validity in this position, it tended to separate God from His created universe and thus brought about a duality of *heaven and earth.* It overlooked the fact that when God had completed His creation He pronounced it "very good" (Gen. 1:31), or a perfect universe. When humanity fell and subjected their God-given realms to futility (Rom. 8:20), humanity and their realms of natural creation were not abdicated by God. Paul states that the natural creation was "subjected to futility . . . *in hope* that the creation itself also will be set free from its slavery to corruption into the freedom of the [redemptive] glory of the children of God" (Rom. 8:20-21). Thus in spite of the Fall and its effects upon the created natural universe there remains *hope* for its redemption and restoration to its original perfection.

God did not give up His sovereignty over the created universe on the occasion of the tragic Fall. He remained the sovereign ruler of the universe and the God of history. In His sovereignty He provided a plan of redemption for fallen humanity and all creation. This means that God is not only over and above His created universe, but He is also present in the universe working out His redemptive plan through Jesus Christ, the Holy Spirit and His church. God is both omnipotent (all powerful) and omniscient (all wise). He is both transcendent and immanent in relation to humanity and the universe. This is known in theology as *Christian Theism* in which God is a *personal* God, as also a *personable* God. He is both the sovereign ruler of the universe and the Heavenly Father of the redeemed.

The dualistic view has often resulted in stark pessimism that has led many to think of salvation in terms of an escape from this evil world and a blissful hereafter in heaven above with God, while they await God's final destruction of His hopelessly doomed creation below. This is not the clear teaching of the Bible.

The song writer expresses the opposite of this view beautifully and theologically in his verse, "This Is my Father's World."

This is my Father's world,
    And to my listening ears,
All nature sings, and round me rings
    The music of the spheres.
This is my Father's world:
    I rest me in the thought
Of rocks and trees, of skies and seas;
    His hand the wonders wrought.

This is my Father's world,
    O let me ne'er forget
That though the wrong seems oft so strong;
    Declare their Maker's praise.
This is my Father's world:
    He shines in all that's fair;
In the rustling grass I hear him pass,
    He speaks to me everywhere.

This is my Father's world,
    O let me ne'er forget
That though the wrong seems oft so strong
    God is the Ruler yet.
This is my Father's world:
    The battle is not done;
Jesus who died shall be satisfied,
    And earth and heaven be one.[6]

The other erroneous view is known in modern times as *theological secularism*. While there have always been certain theologians and religious philosophers who have held this position, in recent decades it has become a prevailing philosophy with the radical liberals that has undermined the faith of many in the Bible and orthodox Christian theology. Among the leading advocates of this position in the twentieth century have been Rudolf Bultmann, Paul Tillich, Harvey Cox, Thomas Altizer, William Hamilton, Bishops James Pike and John A. T. Robinson, to mention but a few of the many very influential thinkers of this secularist school of thought.

In essence, the secularists have denied the transcendence of God and have reduced Him to the impersonal all-pervasive divine principle in man and all nature. In the thought of Paul Tillich God is simply "the ground of all being." In this view God has been removed from His throne as a personal divine sovereign and has been reduced to the divine impersonal energy of man and nature. As the first error has overemphasized the transcendence of God, the second has denied His transcendence and made divinity wholly immanent. Dagobert D. Runes has summed up this position as expressed in the philosophy of Henri Bergson (1859-1941) as follows:

> The phrase *élan vital* sums up his vitalistic doctrine that there is an original life force, that it has passed from one generation of living beings to another by way of developed individual organisms, these being the connecting links between the generations.[7]

When properly understood, this secularistic philosophy is simply a modern form of pantheism in which there is no personal God, and nature operates by a blind impersonal evolutionary process.

If both of the foregoing positions are invalid concerning the location of God and heaven, what then are we to conclude?

Indisputably, heaven is where God is, for it is the very character of God that constitutes heaven. If God's presence fills the universe – if He is omnipresent – and if God is love, as the Scriptures declare Him to be (1 John 4:8), then His manifest presence in love constitutes heaven. The poet sang, "Where Jesus is 'tis heaven there," and "With Jesus here below, it is heaven to know my sins forgiven." Paul speaks of "the God and Father of our Lord Jesus Christ, who has blessed us with every spiritual blessing in *the heavenly places in Christ*" (Eph. 1:3). And again the apostle speaks of "the *summing up of all things in Christ, things in the heavens and things upon the earth*" (Eph. 1:10).

Certainly God is as just as He is loving. His love and His justice are but two sides of the same theological coin. If one's relationship with God is right, then one enjoys the presence of His love here and now, and that is in essence heaven. If, on the other hand, one's relationship with God is not right, then that is to experience His justice — and that is hell here and now. The psalmist exclaimed, "The sorrows of hell compassed me about" (Ps. 18:5 KJV), and again he complained, "The sorrows of death compassed me, and the pains of hell gat hold upon me: I found trouble and sorrow" (Ps. 116:3 KJV).

In a certain sense heaven and hell are both *now and not yet — both present and future.* The poet expressed the experience of redeemed man when he sang, "Once heaven seemed a far off place, till Jesus showed His smiling face."

The British scientist and divine, Henry Drummond, expressed it well in his statement, "Except, therefore, a man be born again, he cannot, he simply *cannot* enter the Kingdom of Heaven. For it is perfectly certain — and you will not misunderstand me — that to enter Heaven a man must take it with him."[8]

In like manner A. Seth Pringle-Pattison says,

Eternal life is not a state of existence to follow upon physical death, but an all-satisfying present experience of the love of God in Christ. It is, as the theologians say, participation in the being of the spiritual Christ! This is the eternal life in the midst of time which is claimed by the saints as an immediate experience, one to which considerations of time are, in fact, indifferent, because we are at rest in the present.[9]

George Matheson, hymn writer and divine, expresses this concept meaningfully in his lines in the hymn, "O Love That Wilt Not Let Me Go."

O Cross that liftest up my head,
    I dare not ask to fly from Thee;

I lay in dust life's glory dead,
And from the ground there blossoms red
  Life that shall endless be!

Frederic W. Farrar asks, "Is it [heaven] not a state rather than a place? Is it not a temper rather than a habitation? Is it not *to be something* rather than *to go somewhere?*" He then replies, "Yes, this, this is Heaven.'[10]

It would be less than true to the Bible to deny that heaven is both the present experience of the redeemed on earth and the continuing future hope of the people of God – both an immanent experience and a transcendent hope – both below and above. Heaven is to be with God now and forever.

Concerning the heavenly identity of the redeemed, J. Paterson-Smyth states: "I am still 'I,' the same conscious self through the whole life of Earth and Hades and Heaven, and therefore the *real life,* the *inner life* can still be understood."[11]

Christ himself began His ministry by declaring that "The Kingdom of God is in your midst [mar. 'within you']" (Luke 17:21). Likewise Paul declared that it is "Christ in you, the hope of glory" (Col. 1:27). Heaven, as identified with the kingdom of God, is primarily an inner experience, as also the universal realm and reign of God without. Heaven means relationship with the King and membership in His kingdom. It signifies righteousness of character rather than personal possession. To His followers Jesus said, "Seek first His [God's] kingdom, and His righteousness; and all these things [necessary to life here] shall be added to you" (Matt. 6:33).

Paterson-Smyth states:

Judgment is a sorting according to character. Heaven and Hell are tempers or conditions of character within us. They are not merely places to which God sends us arbitrarily. They are conditions which we make for ourselves . . . . It is character that makes Heaven; it is character that makes

Hell. They are states of mind that begin here, and are continued and developed there.

A man carries the beginning of Heaven and Hell with him, according to the state of his heart. A selfish, godless man cannot have any Heaven so long as he remains selfish and godless. For Heaven consists in forgetting self, and loving God and man with heart and soul.

The joy of Heaven means the inward joy, the joy of character; the joy of goodness; the joy of likeness to the Nature of God. This is the highest joy of all — the only joy worthy of making Heaven for men who are made in the image of God.

Heaven means a state of character rather than a place of residence. Heaven means to be something rather than to go somewhere. But though Heaven means a state of character rather than a place of residence, yet it means a place of residence, too. And though Heaven means to be something rather than to go somewhere, yet it means to go somewhere, too . . . We do not know a great deal about it. The Bible is given to help us to live rightly in this world, not to satisfy curiosity about the other world.

In all ages — in all races — men have speculated about it [Heaven], and their speculations have been largely colored by their characters and temperaments. The Indian placed it in the Happy Hunting Ground. The Greeks placed it in the Islands of the Blest, where warriors rested after the battle. The Northman and the Mussulman had his equally sensual heaven. And many Christians have as foolish notions as anyone else.

What is the fault in all such? That they do not understand what Heaven really means. They think of it as something outside them which anybody could enjoy if he could only get there. They do not understand that Heaven means the joy of being in union with God — that the outward Heaven has no meaning till the inward Heaven has begun in ourselves.[12]

Theologians at one time separated the blessedness of heaven into two categories, namely the *essential* and the *accidental.* By the first they meant that blissful experience of God's personally revealed presence. This was known as the *Beatific Vision.* By the latter — the *accidental* — however, they meant the additional blessings that result from fellowship with other redeemed persons, and the satisfactions derived from service to God and humanity, and the pleasures of their ever-increasing knowledge of God and the riches of His infinite universe. Certainly there is validity in both of these categories as they relate to the heaven-life.

C. F. Butler has expressed the author's position on "Where Is Heaven?" most magnificently in his poem set to music as follows:

> Since Christ my soul from sin set free,
> This world has been a Heav'n to me;
> And 'mid earth's sorrows and its woe,
> 'Tis Heav'n my Jesus here to know.
>
> Once Heaven seemed a far-off place,
> Till Jesus showed His smiling face;
> Now it's begun within my soul,
> 'Twill last while endless ages roll.
>
> What matters where on earth we dwell?
> On mountain top, or in the dell,
> In cottage, or a mansion fair,
> Where Jesus is, 'tis Heaven there.
>
> O hallelujah, yes, 'tis Heav'n,
> 'Tis Heav'n to know my sins forgiv'n;
> On land or sea, what matters where?
> Where Jesus is, 'tis Heaven there.[13]

Thus we conclude that heaven is both the redeemed's experience of God's presence here and now, and the future hope of the redeemed, and that there is continuity between the present experience and the future hope. The present is heaven begun. The future is heaven continued forever.

What Will Be the Character of Heaven?

If heaven is where the Holy Trinity dwells, then of this there is certainty; there will be no sin in heaven. Sin produces darkness, and "God is light, and in Him there is no darkness at all" (1 John 1:5). In the absence of sin and Satan there will be no temptation in the future heaven. The absence of temptation, however, does not abrogate the moral freedom of the redeemed either in the heaven they experience here or hereafter. God neither redeems robots nor does He make robots of the redeemed in this life or the next.

In the clear light and knowledge of heaven there will be no disposition for the redeemed to turn from the wonders of devotion to and worship of the Christ who saved them from the bondage of sin and the horrors of hell. They will see with purified vision the nature and consequences of the sin from which they were saved and the destruction that sin had wrought through the centuries on the human race. They will likewise view in wonderment the infinite love of God expressed in the redemptive death of Christ on Calvary's cross. Theirs will be a love relationship and commitment to God in Christ that will voluntarily seal their devotion to Him forever. And the voluntary nature of that everlasting commitment to Christ will enrich the love relationship between the redeemed and the Redeemer infinitely beyond any involuntary service or worship of anyone deprived of his moral freedom in the future heaven.

Frederic W. Farrar depicts the character of the future heaven, as he sees it, in the following graphic manner:

There life's stains shall have been purged away; and the gold shall be mixed with dross no longer; nor the fine gold dim. There is no slander there; no envy; no hatred; no malice; no lies. There is no murder there, nor wounds, nor war. The filth of drunkenness is not in that city of God. No bleared and blighted crowds, degraded out of the semblance of humanity, crawl like singed moths, round the flaring houses of multiplied temptations. There are no hearts depraved, corrupted, eaten out by lust; no victims of man's brutal selfishness, no witnesses of his utter shame. [14]

Further, Farrar describes the character of the future heaven as a state,

Where there is no moral ugliness; where repulsive squalor, and degraded art, and insane desire, and loathly vice, and pinching selfishness, shall be no more; where boyhood shall not so live as to make its own manhood miserable; where manhood shall not so live as to make old age dishonourable; where old age shall not so live as to make death ghastly. This, this is heaven! [15]

David Gregg envisions the future of the redeemed as a state, where,

Those who enter the other life are endowed with a perfect personality. In the soul there will be no sin, no unbalanced passion, no crippled faculty, no mental nor moral nor spiritual infirmity . . . It will be complete. Then the body will correspond to the soul. It too will be perfect. I believe that perpetual youth is the standard of the body in heaven. Heaven will make us all young. There will be no old age there. The resurrection means rejuvenation. [16]

The apostle says that "we shall be like Him [Christ], because we shall see Him just as He is" (1 John 3:2). Gregg questions, on the basis of this statement,

Does not that mean the loss of the marks of age

and the enjoyment of perpetual youth? The ascension of Christ took place when he was a young man. *He entered heaven at the age of thirty-three.* To be made like him is to be made youthful. It is to be made thirty-three, and to have thirty-three eternized.[17]

The redeemed in heaven will be purified and glorified individuals from this temporal life. That there will be varieties of temperament and character in heaven is beyond question. Certainly they will be exalted to a higher spiritual condition. The redeemed will not, however, lose their temporal identity in the heaven of the hereafter. They will continue to be themselves. They will retain the personal traits of character and individuality that they had in time, but these will be purified, glorified, and exalted in motive and purpose. People are individuals in the present life, and Christ redeems them as individuals. Heaven will be a community of redeemed individuals. Variety in heaven will contribute to its glory and richness. God's entire creation is characterized by variety. Unity in heaven does not require uniformity there, as God does not require uniformity in the present time.

In the future heaven we will know as we are known (1 Cor. 13:12). Were heaven populated with strangers it would not be heaven at all. The anticipation of fellowship and association in heaven with those we have known and loved on earth constitutes one of heaven's greatest attractions as the redeemed face the future. Gregg expresses this challenging hope well when he says,

> If we have reached the truth, then death is a triumph, an ascension, a coronation, an enthronement, that the redeemed may reign forever with God and Christ.
>
> If we have reached the truth, then it is well, eternally well, with our friends who have left us, and we would not call them back. We shall meet

them again and take up life with them anew, freed from all imperfection; we shall live with them in the life-giving presence of Jesus Christ forever and forever.[18]

Will There Be Activity in Heaven?

Concerning the occupation of the redeemed in their present redeemed lives the Bible has much to say. The specific occupations of the redeemed in the future life, as revealed in the Bible, are more inferential than explicit, though certain activities are clearly indicated. The Bible knows nothing of a static future life. On the one hand such a state would be sheer boredom, and thus would not be heaven at all. On the other hand a future static state would render redemption meaningless. It would be redemption for no good or worthy purpose, and all that God does is purposeful. God himself is always active and creative. Jesus said, "My Father is working until now, and I Myself am working" (John 5:17). Mankind created in the *imago dei* could never be inactive and retain any semblance of the divine image. From the outset of creation God gave to humanity an occupation. He placed our progenitors in the midst of the created natural universe with the commission to subdue it, or bring it under their control for their benefit and His glory, and establish an orderly *rule over it* (Gen. 1:24-31). Even after man's Fall God issued His command to Adam to labor productively (Gen. 3:17-19).

If the aim of redemption is to restore humanity and the created universe to its original perfection and purpose in the plan of God, then it is reasonable to suppose that God's original commission of employment will likewise be restored to redeemed and perfected humanity. Anything less than this would be incomplete restoration through redemption, and would render Christ's own redemptive work incomplete and imperfect. In fact there is a sense in which all worthy employment has redemptive qualities for humanity. This is not to say that man works to merit his salvation. That would be "works righteousness," and such is an insult to God as it says in effect that man's work for his salvation is superior to that which Christ did to save humanity. The following couplet expresses well this difference.

> I would not work my soul to save,
>> For that my Lord has done.
> But I would work like any slave,
>> For the love of His dear Son.

In the light of the foregoing, what then do the Scriptures reveal concerning redeemed humanity's occupation in the future heavenly life?

Basically, if the purpose of redemption is to restore humanity and all creation to God's original purpose and perfection as it was before the Fall, then it is reasonable to suppose that the redeemed will continue in their future restored and perfected state what and where they left off at death in the present life. If God's original purpose for His created universe will be restored through Christ's redemptive work, as Paul clearly indicates (Rom. 8:19-21), then it is both reasonable and scriptural to conclude that His purpose and plan for humanity in that restored creation will likewise be restored. This would mean that the future state of humanity and all creation will continue in endless development as God originally planned it to be. In the light of God's infinity, and humanity's finitude, endless progress will be a possibility. Anything less than this would be ultimate stagnation — inertia — and thus all would end in meaninglessness. In fact this would be annihilationism, and such is not a valid conclusion in either reason or Scripture.

Farrar quotes T. Lynch as saying on the future life of the redeemed,

> O for a nearer insight into heaven,
> More knowledge of the glory and the joy

Which there unto the happy souls is given,
Their intercourse, their worship, their employ;
For it is past belief that Christ hath died
Only that we unending psalms may sing;
That all the gain Death's awful curtains hide
In this eternity of antheming—[19]

Again Farrar asks of the future life,
Who knows what radiant ministrations; what infinite activities; what never-ending progress; what immeasurable happiness; what living ecstacies of unimaginable rapture; where all things are lovely, honorable, pure? . . . Christ hath died to give us entrance into such a Heaven as this, we must believe the same Gospel which tells us, not obscurely, that it is not a reward but a continuity, not a change but a development. To *go there* you must *be thus* . . . If we desire Heaven we must seek it here — if we love Heaven we must love it now.[20]

Certainly love, devotion, and worship of the divine Trinity will be the first and chief occupation of the redeemed in the future life. But there will be work also in this future life. Since the gift of God is eternal *life* (Rom. 6:23) there will be activity, as life is always active — life is ever insurgent against inertia. Inertia produces death. Life is characterized by activity directed toward purposeful productivity. The Bible declares that God's servants will serve Him (Rev. 22:3).

Those who live an active, productive life in the present world cannot endure idleness in retirement. Little wonder that the traditional concept of heaven as eternal rest and inactivity has so little, if any, appeal to such individuals.

Indeed the Bible states, ''Blessed are the dead . . . [for] they may rest from their labors'' (Rev. 14:13). It is, however, from *their labors* — from the toilsome burdens and sorrows of this life that they find rest in the future life. There is a difference between *man's labors* and God's service. Jesus said:

Come to Me, all who are weary and heavy laden, and I will give you rest. Take My yoke upon you, and learn from Me, for I am gentle and humble in heart; and YOU SHALL FIND REST FOR YOUR SOULS. *For My yoke is easy, and My load is light* (Matt. 11:28-30).

Thus, there is rest in work when one's energy is the inwrought power of God in the life of the redeemed both here and hereafter. The eagle that soars aloft exerts but little personal energy. It so adjusts its wings as to allow the air currents to carry it along. It rests in flight. Jesus' last words to His disciples were that they would receive the power of the Holy Spirit coming upon them and go forth in that energy to do His service (Acts 1:8).

J. Paterson-Smyth remarks, concerning the service of the redeemed in the future life:

> In eternal, untiring youth and strength we shall be occupied in doing His blessed will, in helping and blessing the wide universe He has made. Who can tell what glorious ministrations, what infinite activities, what endless growth and progress, and lifting up of brethren God has in store for us all through eternity. Thank God for the thought of that joyous work of never-tiring youth and vigour; work of men proudly rejoicing in their strength, helping the weak ones, teaching the ignorant aye![21]

Whittier expresses it well in his lines:

Tender and most compassionate. Never fear,
For Heaven is love, as God Himself is love;
Thy work below shall be thy work above.[22]

Heaven knows no inactivity. Paterson-Smyth expresses the activities of the future life thus:

> We may well believe *that there will be no dead level of attainment,* no dead level of perfection and joy. That would seem to us very uninteresting. If we may judge from God's dealings here and from

the many texts of scripture there will be an infinite variety of attainment, of positions, of character. "In the Father's house there are many [rooms]. . . ." One day the ideal shall become the real. One day we shall have all these things for which God has put the craving in our hearts today.[23]

That there will be self-fulfillment in the future life there can be no reasonable doubt. The talents, the tastes, the abilities, and the aspirations, when redeemed, purified, and directed to the fulfillment of God's will and purpose will be carried over into the future life. They will continue their developments unimpeded by the hindrances of imperfections and the perversions of evil that characterize the present life. That there will be musicians, artists, scientists, agriculturists, technicians, scholars, secretaries, mechanics, merchants, administrators, teachers and thousands of others whose talents have been developed and exercised in the present life will be necessary, if the present writer's thesis is correct that the future life of humanity and the universe will be the present order redeemed, purified, and restored to its original perfection for the fulfillment of God's ultimate plan and purpose.

Of the future of the universe one thing will be unquestionably certain. Jesus Christ, the Redeemer of men and the universe, will be the loving, just, and righteous Ruler. That He will be assisted in the administration of the future restored universe by His redeemed followers the Scriptures declare. Daniel foresaw this future provision and wrote:

But the saints of the Highest One will receive the kingdom and possess the kingdom forever, for all ages to come. . . . until the Ancient of Days came, and judgment was passed in favor of the saints of the Highest One, and the time arrived when the saints took possession of the kingdom. . . . Then the sovereignty, the dominion, and the greatness of all the kingdoms under the whole heaven will be given to the people of the saints of the Highest One; His kingdom will be an everlasting kingdom, and all the dominions will serve and obey Him (Daniel 7:18, 22, 27).

Likewise Christ declared the co-dominion of the redeemed with Him in His future restored kingdom.

And Jesus said to them, "Truly I say to you, that you who have followed Me, in the regeneration when the Son of Man will sit on His glorious throne, you also shall sit upon twelve thrones, judging the twelve tribes of Israel" (Matt. 19:28).

Paul caught this futuristic vision and wrote to the Corinthian Christians, "Do you not know that the saints will judge the world? . . . Do you not know that we shall judge angels?" (1 Cor. 6:2-3).

Jesus seems to have alluded to God's future restored universal rule when He taught His disciples to pray, "Our Father who art in heaven, Hallowed be Thy name. Thy kingdom come. Thy will be done, On earth as it is in heaven" (Matt. 6:9-10). There is little evidence that this petition will ever be answered in the present unregenerate world order. It will be answered in the future restored order.

The future heaven will be characterized by love, for it will be ruled by the King of Love, and it will be populated by a redeemed community of love-motivated people as God originally created humanity before sin entered the world to pervert His glorious creation.

Paterson-Smyth sums up the character of the restored future kingdom of God by saying that there will be

No sorrow there. "They shall hunger no more, neither thirst any more. There shall be no more curse . . . no pain, no sorrow, no crying, for God shall wipe away all tears from their eyes." . . . No sin in Heaven. No sorrow in Heaven. What else do we certainly know? That the essence of the Heavenly life will be love.[24]

Further, this author states:

It shall be a pure and innocent life. All who on earth have been loving, and pure, and whole, and brave, and self-sacrificing, shall be there. . . . One day we shall have all these things for which God has put the craving in our hearts today.[25]

The essence of this heaven is planted in the hearts of Christ's redeemed servants in the present life. In the future restored existence the external restraints will be removed and there will be heaven without as well as heaven within.

Thus it would appear that heaven, as we know it now, glorious as it may be, is but God's temporary provision for the departed redeemed until the final restoration of all things when heaven and earth will again become one under the reign of Christ as King of Kings and Lord of Lords forever.

In light of the foregoing, certain conclusions appear inevitable.

First, nothing of value in God's natural created order, or the divine, humanly achieved values throughout history, will be ultimately lost when God's redemptive plan is completed. Paul seems to support this conclusion in his comprehensive philosophy of God's redemptive plan as expressed in Romans 8:28. If He is Almighty God, then the forces of evil cannot ultimately defeat His redemptive purpose. What He created, and what He commissioned and enabled humanity to achieve in the beginning, must ultimately be restored, purified and perfected for God's future glory and man's good.

Second, if God's universe was *one* before its disruption by the Fall, then it will be restored to its perfection in the completion of the divine redemptive scheme. If Satan, humanity's Fall, and sin were to finally destroy that which Christ's redemptive work did not and could not restore, then the inescapable conclusion is that evil is greater than good, and Christ's redemptive victory would have been incomplete. Such a conclusion Christian faith cannot tolerate.

Following His death and resurrection, and just prior to His ascension, Christ appeared to His disciples by appointment on a mountain in Galilee where He triumphantly announced His complete and final victory over the entire universe, "All authority [Grk. *exousia* = authority, not *dunamis* = physical power] has been given to Me in heaven and on earth" (Matt. 28:18). In this, Christ's final victorious declaration, His redemptive provision for the sin-tainted universe is announced. This was just before His return to His coronation throne at the right hand of the Father on high (Heb. 10:12). Here He will reign until He has put all enemies under His feet (Heb. 2:7-8) – until He, who is "the seed of the woman," will "bruise the head of the serpent" (Gen. 3:15), and the satanically usurped power in God's universe will be forever destroyed, and all creation will be delivered from its bondage as declared by Paul. "The creation itself also will be set free from its slavery to corruption into the freedom of the glory of the [redeemed] children of God" (Rom. 8:21).

Third, however, those redeemed by Christ will have their part in the execution of His universal authority over His redeemed order. Christ declared His disciples to be His witnesses "even to the remotest part of the earth" (Acts 1:8). That He delegates His authority to His followers for their witness to His completed redemptive work is indicated by His command, "go therefore" (Matt. 28:19). However, *something more* than authority is needed if the redeemed are to bear witness to Christ's victory to all the world. That *something more* Christ promised and provides in His gift of the power of His Spirit as recorded by Luke thus: "You shall receive power [Grk. *dunamis* = physical or enabling power] when the Holy Spirit has come upon you; and you shall be My witnesses . . . to the remotest part of the earth" (Acts 1:8).

This promised power was realized on the Day of Pentecost when they, Christ's disciples, were "all filled with the Holy Spirit and began to speak [to witness] . . ." (Acts 2:4). That the Holy Spirit was, as Samuel Chadwick says, the "Other self of the Christ"[26] corresponds to Christ's prior promise, "Lo, I am with you always [or all the days], even to the end of the age" (Matt. 28:20). The extent to which these first-century disciples of Christ understood and executed His command and empowerment to witness is indicated by Paul in Romans 1:8; 16:26 and Colossians 1:6, 23. All of these declarations of Paul fall within the first thirty years after the disciples' empowerment by the Spirit at Pentecost. Thus the witness to the provisions of Christ's universal redemptive accomplishment rests upon those who have appropriated and experienced that redemption — the *dunamis* of God.

Fourth, if this thesis is correct, then Christ will reign, in conjunction with His redeemed followers, until the whole of responsive mankind and the natural created order are restored to the perfection and purpose of God before the Fall disrupted that divine plan and purpose.

In a certain sense, the ultimately restored, purified, and perfected order will be greater than it was before the Fall, for the values achieved through the long redemptive history of humanity will share in that divine redemption and restoration. Only the disvalues and unrepentant humanity will suffer their loss. However, the intricacies of the outworking of God's redemptive plan in its process through the ages may be understood (varied as those understandings may be), ultimately heaven and earth will be restored to a unified everlasting kingdom under the sovereign, righteous rulership of the Christ who made it possible through His redemptive death and resurrection. But with Him, in His restored and unified universe, redeemed mankind will serve in the glorious ongoing of that universe as God originally planned it. There is no room here for the pessimistic conclusions of Bertrand Russell's nihilistic philosophy of "a universe ultimately in ruins."

With Daniel we concur:

The saints of the Highest One will receive the kingdom and possess the kingdom forever, for all ages to come. . . . Then the sovereignty, the dominion, and the greatness of all the kingdoms under the whole heaven will be given to the people of the saints of the Highest One; His kingdom will be an everlasting kingdom, and all the dominions will serve and obey Him" (Dan. 7:18, 27).

John envisioned this renewed and restored universal kingdom of God and His Christ and exclaimed,

I saw a new heaven and a new earth . . . and I saw the holy city, new Jerusalem, coming down out of heaven from God. . . . And I heard a loud voice from the throne, saying, "Behold, the tabernacle of God is among men, and He shall dwell among them, and they shall be His people, and God Himself shall be among them." . . . And He who sits on the throne said, "Behold, I am making all things new." . . . "He who overcomes shall inherit these things, and I will be his God and he will be My son" (Rev. 21:1-7).

God's message to John expresses the thesis of this book, "And He said to me, 'It is done. I am the Alpha and the Omega, the beginning and the end' " (Rev. 21:6). This concept has been eloquently expressed by Lt. Col. Henry Gariepy:

He [Christ] is *Alpha,* the Beginning, the First. What a staggering claim! First — before the empires of Egypt, Babylon, Greece, Rome. First — before the eons of time spoken of by geologists. First — before the solar system, the Milky Way, the Pleiades.

He is *Omega,* the End, the Last. What a blessed assurance. . . . Because Jesus Christ is the End as well as the Beginning, *Omega* as well as *Alpha,* eternal felicity will be the conclusion for His people.

.   .   .   .

We take comfort and courage from this title with its assurance that our times are in the hands of the eternal, our life becomes complete in Him and He is the Lord of our beginnings and endings.[27]

With George Frederick Handel's *Messiah,* we exultantly exclaim:

Hallelujah: for the Lord God omnipotent reigneth. The kingdom of this world is become the kingdom of our Lord, and of his Christ; and he shall reign for ever and ever. King of Kings, and Lord of Lords. Hallelujah![28]

Thus in the final consummation of God's redemptive provision in Christ there will be demonstrated, "Life's Lordship Over Death," the God-given life that overcomes death forever. The Apostle Paul expresses it thus: "No eye has seen, no ear has heard, no mind has conceived what God has prepared for those who love him – but God has revealed it to us by his Spirit" (1 Cor. 2:9-10 NIV).

And with the Apostle John we conclude:

Yes, dear friends, we are already God's children, right now, and we can't even imagine what it is going to be like later on. But we do know this, that when he comes we shall be like him, as a result of seeing him as he really is (1 John 3:2 *The Living Bible*).

End Notes

CHAPTER V

[1]J. Kenneth Grider, *Baker's Dictionary of Theology,* Everett F. Harrison, ed. (Grand Rapids: Baker, 1960), p. 264.

[2]S. S. Curry, *Vocal and Literary Interpretation of the Bible* (Boston: The Expression Company, 1923), p. xix.

[3]William Barclay, *The Acts of the Apostles* (Philadelphia: Westminster Press, 1955), p. 31.

[4]Grider, *Baker's Dictionary of Theology,* p. 264.

[5]Ibid., p. 265.

[6]Maltbie D. Babcock in *Hymns of the Living Faith* (Syracuse, NY: Wesleyan Methodist Publishing Association, 1951), no. 61.

[7]Dagobert D. Runes, *The Dictionary of Philosophy* (New York: Philosophical Library, 1942), p. 37.

[8]Henry Drummond, *The Greatest Thing in the World* (New York: Grosset and Dunlap, n.d.), pp. 23, 24.

[9]A. Seth Pringle-Pattison as quoted by Frederick Kershner in *Horizons of Immortality* (St. Louis: The Bethany Press, 1926), p. 22.

[10]Frederic W. Farrar, *Eternal Hope* (London; Macmillan and Co., 1912), p. 19.

[11]J. Paterson-Smyth, *The Gospel of the Hereafter* (New York: Revell, 1930), p. 201.

[12]Ibid., pp. 202-209, *passim.*

[13]C. F. Butler, "Where Jesus Is, 'Tis Heaven," in *Tabernacle Hymns, Number Four* (Chicago: Tabernacle Publishing Company, 1945), no. 81.

[14]Farrar, *Eternal Hope,* pp. 17, 18.

[15]Ibid., p. 20.

[16]David Gregg, *The Heaven-Life* (New York: Revell, 1895), pp. 55, 56.

[17]Ibid., p. 56.   [18]Ibid., pp. 81, 82.

[19]Farrar, *Eternal Hope,* p. 16.   [20]Ibid., pp. 19-21.

[21]Paterson-Smyth, *The Gospel of the Hereafter,* p. 216.

[22]John Whittier, "The Brothers of Mercy."

[23]Paterson-Smyth, *The Gospel of the Hereafter,* p. 214.

[24]Ibid, p. 212.   [25]Ibid., p. 211.

[26]Samuel Chadwick, *The Way to Pentecost.* (Berne, Indiana: Light and Hope Publications, 1937), p. 21.

[27]Henry Gariepy, *100 Portraits of Christ,* (Wheaton, IL: Scripture Press Publications, Inc.: *Victor Books,* 1987), pp. 19-20.

[28]George Frederick Handel, *Messiah,* Second Part: "The Passion and Resurrection."

BIBLIOGRAPHY

Adam, Karl. *One and Holy.* NY: Sheed and Ward, 1951.

__________ *The Spirit of Catholicism.* NY: Macmillan, 1952.

Anderson, Norman. *The World's Religions.* Grand Rapids, MI: Wm. B. Eerdmans Publishing Co., 1950.

Archer, John Clarke, *Faiths Men Live By.* NY: Thomas Nelson and Sons, 1934.

Attwater, Donald, ed. *A Catholic Dictionary* (A Catholic Encyclopedic Dictionary). NY: Macmillan, 2nd ed., rev., 1949.

Babcock, Maltbie. *Hymns of the Living Faith.* Syracuse, NY: Wesleyan Methodist Publishing Association, 1951.

Barclay, William. *The Revelation of John,* Vols. 1 & 2. Philadelphia, PA: The Westminster Press, 1960.

__________ *The Acts of the Apostles.* Philadelphia, PA: Westminster Press, 1955.

__________ *A Spiritual Autobiography.* Grand Rapids, MI: Eerdmans, 1975.

Boettner, Loraine. *Immortality.* Philadelphia, PA: Presbyterian and Reform Publishing Co., 1956.

Bonhoeffer, Dietrich, Eberhard Bethge, ed. *Ethics.* NY: Macmillan, 1965.

Bright, John. *The Kingdom of God. The Biblical Concept and Its Meaning for Today.* New York–Nashville: Abingdon Press, 1953.

Burtner, Robert W., and Chiles, Robert E., eds. *John Wesley's Theology: A Collection From His Works.* Nashville, TN: Abingdon Press, 1982.

Butler, C. F. *Tabernacle Hymns, Number Four.* Chicago: Tabernacle Publishing Co., 1945.

Buttrick, George Arthur. *The Interpreter's Bible,* Vols. 1-12. New York–Nashville: Abingdon, 1955.

Carnegie, Dale. *Five Minute Biographies.* NY: Permabooks, 1949.

Carter, Chas. W. *The Wesleyan Bible Commentary,* Vol. 6, Hebrews. Peabody, MA: Hendrickson Publishers, rep. 1986.

Chadwick, Samuel. *The Way to Pentecost.* Berne, IN: Light and Hope Publications, 1937.

Charles, R. H. *A Critical History of the Doctrine of the Future Life.* London: A. & C. Black, 1899.

Clarke, Adam. *Clarke's Commentary,* 6 Vols. Nashville: Abingdon-Cokesbury, n.d.

Cullmann, Oscar. *Christ and Time. The Primitive Conception of Time and History.* Philadelphia, PA: rev. ed., 1964.

Davidson, F. ed., *The New Bible Commentary.* Grand Rapids, MI: William B. Eerdmans, 1954.

Deal, William S. *After Death . . . What?* Kansas City, MO: Beacon Hill Press, 1977.

Denzinger, Henry Dominic. *The Sources of Catholic Dogma.* St. Louis: B. Herder Book Co., 1957.

Drummond, Henry. *The Greatest Thing in the World.* NY: Grosset and Dunlap, n.d.

Duewel, Louis J. *The Intermediate State of Existence.* Independence, KS, n.d.

Durant, Will. *The Story of Philosophy.* Garden City, NY: Garden City Publishing Co., 1943.

Ellicott, Charles John, ed. *Ellicott's Commentary on the Whole Bible,* 8 Vols. Grand Rapids, MI: Zondervan, rep. n.d.

Farrar, Frederic W. *Eternal Hope.* London: Macmillan and Co., Ltd., 1912.

Forell, George W. *The Protestant Faith.* Philadelphia: Fortress Press, 1975. Chapter 12, "Eschatology."

Frost, S. E. *The Basic Teachings of the Great Philosophers.* Philadelphia, PA: The Blakiston Co., 1942.

Fuller, B.A.G. *A History of Philosophy.* NY: Henry Holt and Co., 1947.

Gariepy, Henry. *100 Portraits of Christ.* Wheaton, IL: Victor Books. Scripture Press Publications, Inc. 1987.

Garrison, Winfred Ernest. *A Protestant Manifesto.* NY: Abingdon-Cokesbury Press, 1952.

Gerstner, John H. *The Theology of the Major Sects.* Grand Rapids, MI: Baker Book House, 1960.

Glenn, Paul J. *An Introduction to Philosophy.* St. Louis, MO: Herder Book Company, 1944.

Gregg, David. *The Heaven Life,* or *Stimulus for Two Worlds.* NY: Revell, 1895.

Grider, J. Kenneth, and Harrison, Everett F., eds. *Baker's Dictionary of Theology.* Grand Rapids, MI: Baker Book House, 1960.

Guardini, Romano. *The Faith and Modern Man.* NY: Pantheon Books, 1952.

__________. *The Last Things.* NY: Pantheon Books, 1954.

Henry, A. M. *Theological Library, The Historical and Mystical Christ.* Chicago: Fidec Publishers Association, 1958.

Hopfe, Lewis M. *Religions of the World.* New York–London: Macmillan Publishing Co. and Collier Macmillan Publishers, 1987.

Kershner, Frederick D. *Horizons of Immortality.* St. Louis, MO: The Bethany Press, 1926.

Keyser, Leander S. *A System of General Ethics.* Burlington, IA: The Lutheran Literary Board, 1934.

Koing, Adrio. *The Eclipse of Christ in Eschatology: Toward a Christ Centered Approach.* Grand Rapids, MI: William B. Eerdmans, 1988.

Ladd, Eldon. *The Blessed Hope.* Grand Rapids, MI: William B. Eerdmans Publishing Co., 1956.

————— *The Last Things.* Grand Rapids, MI: William B. Eerdmans Publishing Co., 1975.

Literary Board of the Lutheran Church (Missouri Synod). *The Life That Never Ends: Funeral Sermons.* St. Louis: Concordia Publishing House, 1949.

MacGregor, Geddes. *Introduction to Religious Philosophy.* Boston: Houghton Mifflin, 1959.

Martin, Walter R. *The Kingdom of the Cults.* Minneapolis, MN: Bethany House Publishing Co., 1968.

Maurice, Frederick Denison. *Theological Essays.*

Minear, Paul S. *New Testament Apocalyptic.* Nashville, TN: Abingdon Press, 1988.

Morris, Leon. *Apocalyptic.* Grand Rapids, MI: Wm. B. Eerdmans Publishing Co., 1972.

Orr, James. *International Standard Bible Encyclopedia.* Vols. 1-6. Grand Rapids, MI: Wm. B. Eerdmans Publishing Co., rep. 1957.

Pache, René. *The Future Life.* Chicago: Moody Press, 1962.

Paterson-Smyth, J. *The Gospel of the Hereafter.* NY: Revell, 1930.

Poe, Edgar Allen. "The Raven." *One Hundred and One Famous Poems.* Chicago: The Cable Co., 1929.

Ramm, Bernard. *The Christian View of Science and the Scriptures.* Grand Rapids, MI: Wm. B. Eerdmans Publishing Co., 1954.

Runes, Dagobert. *The Dictionary of Philosophy.* NY: Philosophical Library, 1942.

Russell, Bertrand, *Selected Papers of Bertrand Russell.* NY: Random House, The Modern Library, 1927.

Ryrie, Charles C. *The Final Countdown.* Wheaton, IL: The Scripture Press, 1988.

Schmithals, W. "Death," *The New International Dictionary of New Testament Theology.* Colin Brown, Gen. Ed. Grand Rapids, MI: Zondervan, 1975.

Schmitt, Abraham. *Dialogue With Death.* Waco, TX: Word Books, 1976.

Smith, Timothy L., et al. *Contemporary Wesleyan Theology.* Vol. 2. Charles W. Carter, Gen. Ed. Grand Rapids, MI: Zondervan Publishing House, 1983, Chapter 22, Hymnology: "The Theology of the Wesleyan Hymns."

Taylor, Richard S. et al. eds. *Beacon Dictionary of Theology.* Kansas City, MO: Beacon Hill Press, 1983.

Tenney, Merrill. ed. *Zondervan Pictorial Encyclopedia of the Bible.* 5 Vols. Grand Rapids, MI: Zondervan Publishing House.

Titus, Harold H. *Living Issues in Philosophy.* NY: Van Nostrand-Reinhold Co., 1970.

Trueblood, David Elton. *Philosophy of Religion.* Grand Rapids, MI: Baker Book House, 1975.

Van Baalan, Karl. *The Chaos of the Cults.* Grand Rapids, MI: Wm. B. Eerdmans Publishing Co., n.d.

Van Gemeren, William. *The Progress of Redemption: The Story of Salvation from Creation to the New Jerusalem.* Grand Rapids, MI: Zondervan Publishing Company, 1988.

Wesley, John. *Explanatory Notes Upon the New Testament.* London: The Epworth Press. rep. 1954.

__________. *Explanatory Notes Upon the Old Testament.* 3 vols. Salem, OH: Schmul Publishers, rep. 1975.

__________. *A Plain Account of Christian Perfection.* Louisville, KY: Pentecostal Publishing Co., n.d.

Whittier, John Greenleaf. *The Complete Poetical Works of John Greenleaf Whittier.* Boston: Houghton Mifflin & Co., 1884.

Wynkoop, Mildred Bangs. *Foundation of Wesleyan Arminian Theology.* Kansas City, MO: Beacon Hill Press, 1967.

Continued from back cover

In his latest book, *Life's Lordship Over Death* Dr. Charles W. Carter has made a valuable contribution to this unusual subject. He shows a thorough knowledge of relevant biblical, philosophical and theological material.

Not much attention is given today to the subject of "Personal Existence After Physical Death," the title of his second chapter. Some people have become rightly concerned about the fact that for many years we have heard very little preaching about hell and so sinners do not dread their fate. Dr. Carter covers this field very carefully. He even adds a chapter (III) on "The Doctrine of Purgatory," to warn against false ideas still circulating on that subject. We do not recall having read a book that treats life after death so thoroughly and helpfully as this book does. The author goes on to treat immortality and heaven in the last two chapters. His discussion of both hell and heaven is very exciting to read – *an unusual book.*

> Ralph Earle
> Professor Emeritus of New Testament
> Nazarene Theological Seminary

Reading *Life's Lordship Over Death* was an interesting, thought-provoking and enriching experience. In fact, it represents the kind of study which should not be quickly read but rather thoughtfully considered and analyzed for the broadening of our understanding of those things presently and eventually of major importance to all of us. I should like to see it made generally available and would pray that it shall be in the libraries of thoughtful Christians of both the ministry and laity.

> J. D. Abbott
> General Superintendent Emeritus
> The Wesleyan Church

This book, well organized and genuinely helpful, will enjoy an attentive and appreciative readership. Moreover, Dr. Carter's enriching knowledge, both of Christian and non-Christian beliefs, commends itself to pastors and teachers, professional and lay persons. The range of treatment brings into view related concerns, adding merit to the book. Best of all, the clear Christian truth of eternal life comes through with power and persuasion.

> Donald E. Demaray
> Fisher Professor of Preaching
> Asbury Theological Seminary